Holistic Wellness

Whole Wellness & Wonderful Well-being

By Sydney Brown

Holistic Wellness

WHOLE WELLNESS & WONDERFUL WELL-BEING

by Sydney Brown

Published by TLM Publishing House

5905 Atlanta Highway, Alpharetta GA.
https://www.ttpublishinghouse.com
Copyright © 2023 TLM Publishing House

Legal Disclaimer: We utilized ChatGPT for help with research. We are making no claims, whether medical, financial, or otherwise.

Contents

Introduction

In today's fast-paced world, where quick solutions often overshadow in-depth understanding, "Whole Wellness & Wonderful Well-being" offers readers a glimpse into the enriching realm of holistic living. This book doesn't claim to be an exhaustive guide but rather an illuminating introduction, shedding light on the myriad holistic options available to those seeking a more integrated approach to well-being.

Every chapter within these pages brings to life a facet of the holistic philosophy, underscoring the belief that our well-being isn't just physical. True health and happiness flourish when we harmoniously blend our emotional, mental, and spiritual dimensions.

"Whole Wellness & Wonderful Well-being" is an invitation to explore the vast landscape of holistic practices and principles. It encourages readers to find balance in their lives, not by striving for an unattainable ideal but by gaining awareness of the choices that resonate with their inner selves.

1

This holistic perspective isn't just a lifestyle trend; it's a lens through which we can view the world. It reminds us that every decision we make, from the food we consume to the thoughts we nurture, has an impact—on ourselves, our communities, and the world at large.

As you journey through the curated insights of "Whole Wellness & Wonderful Well-being", you'll discover a variety of practices and philosophies that can enrich your personal path to wellness. Whether you're new to the concept of holistic living or already familiar with some of its tenets, this book offers valuable perspectives, encouraging you to delve deeper and explore the holistic options that resonate with you.

Welcome to an enlightening exploration of holistic living. Let "Whole Wellness & Wonderful Well-being" be your introductory guide to a world of balance, harmony, and holistic well-being.

Holistic Addiction Recovery: A Comprehensive Approach to Healing the Mind, Body, and Spirit

Holistic addiction recovery is a holistic and multidimensional approach to treating addiction that recognizes the interconnection of the mind, body, and spirit. It goes beyond addressing the symptoms of addiction and delves into the underlying causes and imbalances that contribute to addictive behaviors. This comprehensive approach emphasizes healing on all levels to achieve long-lasting recovery. In this book, we will explore the principles, methods, benefits, and the significance of holistic addiction recovery in addressing the complex nature of addiction.

Principles of Holistic Addiction Recovery

Mind-Body-Spirit Connection: Holistic addiction recovery is based on the belief that the mind, body, and spirit are interconnected, and imbalances in any of these areas can contribute to addictive behaviors. Treating addiction requires addressing each of these dimensions.

Individualized Care: Holistic recovery recognizes that each person's addiction is unique and complex, requiring a personalized treatment plan that considers their physical, emotional, and spiritual needs.

Root Cause Exploration: Rather than merely treating the symptoms of addiction, holistic recovery seeks to uncover and address the root causes, which may include trauma, unresolved emotions, or spiritual disconnection.

Natural Healing: Holistic addiction recovery often incorporates natural and alternative therapies to support healing, including nutrition, mindfulness, meditation, yoga, acupuncture, and more.

Methods and Techniques

Holistic Therapies: A wide range of holistic therapies, such as acupuncture, chiropractic care, massage therapy, and herbal medicine, are employed to address physical imbalances and promote overall health.

Mindfulness and Meditation: These practices help individuals develop greater self-awareness, manage cravings, and reduce stress, which can trigger addictive behaviors.

Nutrition and Exercise: Proper nutrition and regular physical activity are essential components of holistic recovery, helping to repair the body and maintain a balanced mood.

Emotional Healing: Various therapeutic approaches, including cognitive-behavioral therapy (CBT) and dialectical behavior therapy (DBT), help individuals address emotional issues and learn healthier coping mechanisms.

Spiritual Connection: Spiritual practices, such as prayer, meditation, and connecting with nature, help individuals develop a deeper sense of purpose and meaning.

Benefits of Holistic Addiction Recovery

Comprehensive Healing: Holistic addiction recovery addresses the multifaceted nature of addiction, leading to more comprehensive and lasting recovery.

Personal Empowerment: Individuals in holistic recovery become active participants in their healing journey, taking responsibility for their physical, emotional, and spiritual well-being.

Reduced Relapse: By identifying and addressing the root causes of addiction and using holistic therapies, individuals are better equipped to prevent relapse.

Improved Overall Well-Being: Holistic recovery often leads to better physical health, emotional stability, and an increased sense of spiritual connection, resulting in improved overall well-being.

Enhanced Self-Awareness: Holistic practices encourage self-reflection and greater self-awareness, helping individuals gain insights into their addictive behaviors and make positive changes.

The Significance of Holistic Addiction Recovery

Holistic addiction recovery has gained recognition and significance for several reasons:

Addressing Underlying Causes: Traditional addiction treatment often focuses on symptom management. Holistic recovery delves deeper, targeting the underlying causes and contributors to addiction.

Empowering Individuals: Holistic recovery empowers individuals to take an active role in their healing process, promoting self-awareness, self-empowerment, and personal growth.

Preventing Relapse: By addressing the physical, emotional, and spiritual aspects of addiction, holistic recovery equips individuals with better tools to prevent relapse and maintain long-term sobriety.

Supporting Overall Health: Holistic recovery has the added benefit of improving overall health, enhancing mental and physical well-being, and promoting balance in all aspects of life.

Holistic addiction recovery offers a comprehensive and integrated approach to healing addiction by recognizing the interconnectedness of the mind, body, and spirit. By addressing the root causes of addiction and promoting personal empowerment, it empowers individuals to achieve lasting recovery.

This holistic approach is significant for its potential to provide comprehensive healing and prevent relapse while enhancing overall well-being and personal growth.

Holistic Astrology: Exploring the Multidimensional Aspects of Astrological Understanding

Holistic astrology is a comprehensive approach to astrology that delves into the interconnected nature of the physical, mental, emotional, and spiritual aspects of an individual's life. This perspective recognizes that astrology is not merely a tool for predicting future events but a means of understanding the whole person, including their physical well-being, mental and emotional states, and spiritual evolution. In this book, we will explore the principles, methodologies, and benefits of holistic astrology, highlighting the significance of its multidimensional approach.

Principles of Holistic Astrology

Interconnectedness: Holistic astrology is founded on the principle that every aspect of an individual's life is interconnected. Events in one area of life can affect other areas, and the natal chart reflects these connections.

Balance and Harmony: The goal of holistic astrology is to help individuals achieve balance and harmony in all areas of life, fostering a state of holistic well-being.

Personal Growth: Holistic astrology emphasizes personal growth and spiritual evolution, encouraging individuals to learn and grow from their experiences.

Empowerment: Rather than being predictive, holistic astrology empowers individuals to make conscious choices, navigate life's challenges, and evolve spiritually.

Methods and Techniques

Natal Chart Analysis: Holistic astrology starts with a comprehensive analysis of the natal chart, which is a personalized map of the positions of the planets at the time of an individual's birth.

Psychological Astrology: Psychological astrology explores the mental and emotional aspects of a person's life, helping individuals understand their inner workings and emotional patterns.

Medical Astrology: Medical astrology examines the astrological influences on physical health and well-being, identifying potential health issues and suitable treatments.

Spiritual Astrology: Spiritual astrology focuses on the individual's spiritual path, highlighting their soul's purpose and evolution throughout their lifetime.

Transit Analysis: Holistic astrologers analyze planetary transits and progressions to provide insights into the timing of significant life events and the growth opportunities they present.

Benefits of Holistic Astrology

Self-Discovery: Holistic astrology aids in self-discovery, providing a deep understanding of one's personality, desires, challenges, and life's purpose.

Improved Relationships: By understanding their own and others' astrological influences, individuals can enhance their relationships and communication.

Physical Well-Being: Medical astrology helps individuals become aware of their physical vulnerabilities, allowing them to take preventive measures for better health.

Emotional Well-Being: Psychological astrology assists in identifying and addressing emotional patterns and trauma, promoting emotional healing.

Spiritual Growth: Holistic astrology guides individuals on their spiritual journey, helping them align with their soul's purpose and find meaning in life.

The Significance of Holistic Astrology

Holistic astrology is significant for several reasons:

Comprehensive Understanding: It provides a comprehensive understanding of an individual's life, covering the physical, mental, emotional, and spiritual dimensions.

Empowerment: Holistic astrology empowers individuals to take control of their lives and make conscious choices, rather than feeling at the mercy of external forces.

Balance and Harmony: It promotes balance and harmony, allowing individuals to cultivate a more fulfilling and harmonious life.

Personal Growth: Holistic astrology encourages personal growth and spiritual evolution, helping individuals learn from their experiences and challenges.

Holistic astrology is a multidimensional approach that recognizes the interconnectedness of the physical, mental, emotional, and spiritual aspects of an individual's life.

By exploring an individual's natal chart, psychological and emotional patterns, physical health influences, and spiritual evolution, holistic astrology provides a comprehensive understanding of the whole person.

This approach is significant for its capacity to empower individuals, promote balance and harmony, and foster personal growth and spiritual development.

Holistic Beauty Retreats: Embracing Natural and Wholesome Beauty Practices

Holistic beauty retreats are immersive getaways that emphasize natural and holistic beauty practices to promote overall well-being and self-care. These retreats provide a sanctuary where individuals can rejuvenate, relax, and nourish their bodies, minds, and spirits.

By focusing on natural, sustainable, and holistic approaches to beauty and self-care, participants can achieve a harmonious and radiant sense of beauty from within. In this book, we will delve into the principles, elements, benefits, and significance of holistic beauty retreats, which provide a rejuvenating escape from the stresses of everyday life.

Principles of Holistic Beauty Retreats

Holistic Wellness: Holistic beauty retreats follow the holistic wellness approach, recognizing the interconnectedness of physical, emotional, and spiritual well-being. They aim to promote a balanced and harmonious lifestyle.

Natural Beauty: The primary focus is on embracing and enhancing one's natural beauty, nurturing the skin, hair, and body without the use of harsh chemicals or invasive procedures.

Self-Care and Mindfulness: These retreats emphasize the importance of self-care, mindfulness, and stress reduction as integral components of beauty and overall well-being.

Sustainable Practices: Holistic beauty retreats often promote eco-friendly and sustainable beauty products and practices to minimize the impact on the environment.

Elements of Holistic Beauty Retreats

Natural Skincare and Body Treatments: Retreats offer organic and natural skincare products and treatments, including facials, body scrubs, and massages, using ingredients such as essential oils, herbs, and botanical extracts.

Yoga and Meditation: Holistic beauty retreats often incorporate yoga and meditation sessions to promote inner peace, reduce stress, and enhance physical and mental well-being.

Healthy Nutrition: Participants are provided with nourishing, plant-based meals that support radiant skin, healthy hair, and overall vitality. These meals are often based on organic and locally sourced ingredients.

Workshops and Seminars: Retreats offer educational sessions on topics like natural skincare, nutrition, mindfulness, and self-care techniques to help participants incorporate holistic beauty practices into their daily lives.

Outdoor Activities: Many holistic beauty retreats take place in serene natural settings, allowing attendees to connect with nature through activities like hiking, forest bathing, and outdoor meditation.

Benefits of Holistic Beauty Retreats

Nourished and Radiant Skin: The use of natural and organic skincare products, coupled with a healthy diet, can result in nourished, glowing skin.

Stress Reduction: Retreats emphasize relaxation and mindfulness practices that can lead to stress reduction and enhanced emotional well-being.

Sustainable Beauty: Holistic beauty retreats encourage the use of eco-friendly and sustainable beauty products and practices, promoting environmental consciousness.

Mind-Body Connection: Yoga, meditation, and outdoor activities help foster a strong mind-body connection, improving overall health and well-being.

Improved Self-Care: Participants learn self-care practices and techniques that can be integrated into their daily lives, promoting long-term well-being.

Significance of Holistic Beauty Retreats

Self-Care and Empowerment: Holistic beauty retreats empower individuals to take control of their well-being by teaching self-care practices that extend beyond the retreat experience.

Enhanced Self-Confidence: Nurturing the mind, body, and spirit contributes to enhanced self-confidence, as individuals feel more comfortable and content with themselves.

Sustainable Beauty: By focusing on eco-friendly and natural beauty practices, holistic beauty retreats promote a more sustainable approach to beauty.

Inner Beauty: These retreats emphasize the significance of inner beauty, reminding participants that true beauty radiates from within and extends to the physical body.

Holistic beauty retreats offer an opportunity to embrace natural, sustainable, and holistic beauty practices while promoting overall well-being. By nurturing the mind, body, and spirit through organic skincare, healthy nutrition, self-care techniques, and mindfulness practices, participants can achieve a harmonious sense of beauty from within. Holistic beauty retreats hold significance in promoting sustainable beauty, enhancing self-confidence, and fostering a deeper connection with one's inner beauty.

Holistic Beauty: Nurturing Your Natural Radiance with Non-Toxic Skincare Practices

Holistic beauty is a philosophy and approach to beauty and skincare that emphasizes the use of natural, non-toxic, and sustainable products and practices to enhance and maintain your beauty while promoting overall well-being.

This holistic perspective recognizes the interconnectedness of physical, emotional, and spiritual health, and it encourages individuals to embrace a beauty routine that respects their bodies and the environment.

In this book, we will explore the principles, methods, benefits, and the significance of holistic beauty, which encourages a radiant, natural glow that goes beyond the skin's surface.

Principles of Holistic Beauty

Mind-Body-Spirit Connection: Holistic beauty embraces the idea that beauty is not just skin deep; it is deeply intertwined with our physical, emotional, and spiritual well-being.

Non-Toxic Ingredients: A fundamental principle of holistic beauty is the use of non-toxic ingredients in skincare and beauty products, avoiding harmful chemicals, synthetic fragrances, and harsh additives.

Sustainable and Eco-Friendly: Holistic beauty advocates for sustainable and eco-friendly practices, including the use of recyclable packaging and cruelty-free products.

Self-Care and Mindfulness: Taking a holistic approach to beauty involves self-care practices and mindfulness techniques that promote relaxation and reduce stress, ultimately contributing to radiant skin.

Methods and Techniques of Holistic Beauty

Non-Toxic Skincare: Holistic beauty prioritizes skincare products free from harmful chemicals, embracing natural ingredients like plant-based oils, herbs, and essential oils.

Healthy Nutrition: A nutritious, plant-based diet full of antioxidants, vitamins, and minerals nourishes the skin from the inside out, contributing to a healthy and radiant complexion.

Mindful Practices: Meditation, yoga, and mindfulness exercises reduce stress, promoting a healthy mind and skin. Stress can exacerbate skin issues like acne and premature aging.

Non-Invasive Techniques: Holistic beauty advocates for non-invasive treatments such as facial massages, gua sha, and lymphatic drainage to promote healthy, radiant skin.

Natural Makeup: Choosing natural and non-toxic makeup products, free from synthetic dyes and fragrances, reduces the potential for skin irritations and allergic reactions.

Benefits of Holistic Beauty

Healthier Skin: Non-toxic, natural skincare promotes healthier, radiant skin while minimizing the risk of irritation, allergies, and other skin issues.

Non-Toxic Lifestyle: By using non-toxic beauty products, you reduce your exposure to harmful chemicals and contribute to a healthier and more sustainable lifestyle.

Mind-Body Balance: Holistic beauty practices promote a balanced and harmonious state of mind and body, contributing to overall well-being.

Environmental Consciousness: Sustainable beauty practices support eco-friendly initiatives and minimize the environmental impact of the beauty industry.

Inner Beauty: Holistic beauty emphasizes that true beauty radiates from within and that a healthy and balanced body and mind contribute to outer radiance.

The Significance of Holistic Beauty

Self-Care and Empowerment: Holistic beauty encourages self-care practices and mindfulness techniques, empowering individuals to take control of their well-being.

Non-Toxic Living: Embracing non-toxic beauty practices reduces the risk of skin irritations and long-term health issues associated with harmful chemicals.

Mind-Body Balance: Holistic beauty reinforces the connection between physical, emotional, and spiritual well-being, promoting overall harmony.

Sustainable Beauty: By choosing sustainable and eco-friendly beauty products, you contribute to the preservation of the environment and a more conscious way of living.

Holistic beauty is a wholesome and eco-conscious approach to beauty and skincare that values non-toxic ingredients, self-care practices, and mindfulness. By nurturing your body, mind, and spirit through natural skincare, healthy nutrition, and stress-reduction techniques, you can achieve radiant, natural beauty while promoting overall well-being.

Holistic beauty is significant for its holistic approach to beauty, which emphasizes a healthy, balanced mind, body, and spirit, as well as its contribution to a more sustainable and environmentally conscious way of living.

Holistic Birth Support: A Comprehensive Approach to Pregnancy and Childbirth

Holistic birth support is a comprehensive approach to pregnancy and childbirth that focuses on nurturing the mind, body, and spirit of expectant parents. This approach acknowledges the interconnected nature of pregnancy, birth, and the well-being of both the parents and the baby. Holistic birth support extends beyond traditional medical care, emphasizing natural and holistic practices that empower expectant mothers and fathers to have a positive and healthy birthing experience. In this book, we will explore the principles, methods, benefits, and significance of holistic birth support, which aims to provide comprehensive care and emotional support during this significant life event.

Principles of Holistic Birth Support

Holistic Well-Being: Holistic birth support recognizes the importance of the mind, body, and spirit in the pregnancy and birthing process. It aims to achieve balance and harmony in these aspects.

Natural and Non-Invasive: Holistic birth support emphasizes natural, non-invasive, and drug-free approaches to pregnancy and childbirth, prioritizing practices that minimize medical interventions.

Informed Decision-Making: This approach encourages expectant parents to be informed about their birthing options, empowering them to make decisions that align with their beliefs and values.

Emotional and Spiritual Support: Holistic birth support provides emotional and spiritual care, acknowledging the significance of these aspects in the birthing process.

Methods and Techniques of Holistic Birth Support

Prenatal Education: Holistic birth support often includes prenatal education classes that cover various aspects of pregnancy, childbirth, and parenting. These classes provide information about different birthing options, techniques, and approaches.

Mindfulness and Relaxation: Techniques like mindfulness, meditation, deep breathing, and relaxation exercises are taught to help manage stress and anxiety during pregnancy and labor.

Natural Pain Management: Holistic birth support emphasizes non-pharmacological pain management techniques such as hydrotherapy, massage, and movement to ease labor pain.

Emotional Support: Doulas, midwives, or other holistic birth support professionals offer emotional support to expectant parents, providing reassurance and encouragement throughout the birthing process.

Spiritual Connection: For those who value spiritual aspects in childbirth, holistic birth support may incorporate practices like prayer, guided visualization, and rituals to enhance the spiritual experience.

Benefits of Holistic Birth Support

Empowerment: Expectant parents are empowered to make informed decisions about their birthing experience, fostering a sense of control and confidence.

Less Medical Intervention: Holistic birth support often results in fewer medical interventions during labor, reducing the potential for complications and unnecessary procedures.

Reduced Stress: Stress and anxiety are managed more effectively through mindfulness and relaxation techniques, promoting a calmer and more comfortable birthing experience.

Enhanced Bonding: The emotional and spiritual aspects of holistic birth support can strengthen the bond between parents and the newborn.

Positive Birth Experience: Holistic birth support contributes to a more positive and fulfilling birthing experience, often associated with shorter labor and fewer complications.

The Significance of Holistic Birth Support

Personalized Care: Holistic birth support is tailored to the individual needs and beliefs of expectant parents, providing a personalized and meaningful birthing experience.

Empowerment and Autonomy: It empowers parents to actively participate in the birthing process and make decisions that align with their values.

Natural and Holistic Approach: Holistic birth support promotes natural and holistic approaches to childbirth, which can result in better outcomes for both the mother and the baby.

Emotional and Spiritual Well-Being: The emotional and spiritual support provided through this approach contributes to a more fulfilling birthing experience, enhancing the overall well-being of the family.

Holistic birth support is a comprehensive approach to pregnancy and childbirth that prioritizes the well-being of the expectant parents and the baby. By providing natural, non-invasive, and holistic practices, emotional and spiritual support, and personalized care, holistic birth support empowers parents to have a positive and healthy birthing experience. Its significance lies in its emphasis on holistic well-being, informed decision-making, and emotional and spiritual care, all of which contribute to a meaningful and fulfilling birthing experience.

Holistic Business Coaching: Aligning Entrepreneurship with Holistic Values

Holistic business coaching is a comprehensive approach to entrepreneurship that aims to guide individuals in aligning their business practices with holistic values.

In this context, holistic refers to considering the interconnectedness of various aspects of a business, including the well-being of the entrepreneur, employees, clients, and the environment.

Holistic business coaching goes beyond traditional business strategies and incorporates mindful, sustainable, and ethical practices.

In this book, we will explore the principles, methods, benefits, and significance of holistic business coaching, emphasizing its role in fostering a business environment that is not only profitable but also promotes overall well-being and ethical business practices.

Principles of Holistic Business Coaching

Interconnectedness: Holistic business coaching recognizes that every aspect of a business, from the entrepreneur's well-being to the company's impact on the environment, is interconnected.

Ethical Business Practices: Holistic values in business coaching promote ethical and socially responsible practices that prioritize the well-being of employees, clients, and the community.

Mindful Leadership: Holistic business coaching emphasizes mindful leadership that includes self-awareness, self-care, and a commitment to fostering a positive work environment.

Sustainable Growth: Holistic values promote sustainable growth that minimizes harm to the environment and benefits future generations.

Methods and Techniques of Holistic Business Coaching

Business Assessment: Holistic business coaching often begins with an assessment of the entrepreneur's current business practices, values, and objectives.

Mindful Leadership Training: Entrepreneurs are taught to develop self-awareness, emotional intelligence, and resilience to become mindful and ethical leaders.

Ethical Decision-Making: Coaching includes guidance on making ethical business decisions that align with holistic values.

Employee Well-Being: Holistic business coaching fosters a culture of employee well-being by providing training in stress management, work-life balance, and promoting a positive workplace environment.

Sustainability Practices: Coaches encourage the integration of sustainable and environmentally friendly business practices to reduce the company's environmental impact.

Benefits of Holistic Business Coaching

Ethical Reputation: Businesses that align with holistic values tend to have a better reputation, which can lead to increased trust among clients and stakeholders.

Employee Satisfaction: Holistic values create a positive work environment, resulting in happier, more engaged employees who are more likely to stay with the company.

Personal Growth: Entrepreneurs often experience personal growth and self-improvement through holistic business coaching, contributing to their overall well-being.

Environmental Responsibility: Businesses that incorporate sustainable practices in their operations contribute to a healthier environment and community.

Long-Term Success: Holistic business practices can lead to long-term success by creating a loyal customer base, fostering innovation, and reducing costs through sustainable practices.

The Significance of Holistic Business Coaching

Well-Being: Holistic business coaching contributes to the overall well-being of entrepreneurs, employees, clients, and the community by promoting ethical practices and mindful leadership.

Ethical Business: It is significant in fostering ethical business practices that align with societal expectations and contribute to a positive and sustainable future.

Environmental Responsibility: Holistic business coaching plays a crucial role in encouraging environmentally responsible practices in the business world, which is essential for the health of our planet.

Holistic Growth: Holistic business coaching supports the growth of the business, both in terms of profits and overall well-being, by fostering a sustainable and ethical approach to entrepreneurship.

Holistic business coaching is a valuable approach to entrepreneurship that prioritizes ethical and sustainable business practices. By emphasizing interconnectedness, ethical decision-making, employee well-being, and sustainability, it contributes to the well-being of entrepreneurs, employees, clients, and the community. Its significance lies in its potential to foster ethical business practices, environmental responsibility, and holistic growth in the business world.

Holistic business coaching not only promotes profitability but also aims to create a positive and sustainable future for all stakeholders involved.

Holistic Coaching: Nurturing Personal Growth and Transformation

Holistic coaching is a comprehensive and integrated approach to personal development and transformation that emphasizes the interconnectedness of various aspects of an individual's life.

It goes beyond traditional coaching methods by addressing not only professional goals but also personal, emotional, and spiritual well-being.

Holistic coaching aims to guide individuals in achieving a balanced and harmonious life, fostering personal growth, and helping them tap into their full potential. In this book, we will explore the principles, methods, benefits, and the significance of holistic coaching in supporting personal growth and transformation.

Principles of Holistic Coaching

Holistic Well-Being: Holistic coaching is based on the principle that an individual's overall well-being encompasses physical, emotional, mental, and spiritual dimensions. It recognizes that all these aspects are interconnected.

Balance and Harmony: Holistic coaching seeks to help individuals achieve balance and harmony in their lives, fostering personal growth and transformation.

Self-Discovery: It emphasizes self-awareness, self-discovery, and self-improvement as integral components of personal growth and transformation.

Mind-Body-Spirit Connection: Holistic coaching acknowledges the mind-body-spirit connection and encourages individuals to explore their spiritual and emotional selves.

Methods and Techniques of Holistic Coaching

Goal Setting: Holistic coaching begins with goal setting, addressing not only professional goals but also personal aspirations, emotional growth, and spiritual well-being.

Mindfulness and Self-Reflection: Techniques like mindfulness, meditation, and journaling are used to foster self-awareness and self-reflection.

Emotional Intelligence: Holistic coaching often involves developing emotional intelligence to better understand and manage emotions.

Self-Care Practices: Holistic coaching incorporates self-care practices, such as exercise, nutrition, and stress management, to enhance physical and emotional well-being.

Spiritual Exploration: Individuals are encouraged to explore their spiritual beliefs, values, and practices, fostering a deeper connection with their inner selves.

Benefits of Holistic Coaching

Personal Growth: Holistic coaching promotes personal growth by helping individuals tap into their potential, develop self-awareness, and enhance their overall well-being.

Improved Well-Being: It contributes to improved physical, emotional, and spiritual well-being, leading to a more balanced and harmonious life.

Stress Reduction: Holistic coaching provides tools for stress reduction, leading to a calmer and more centered life.

Enhanced Self-Awareness: It encourages self-awareness and self-reflection, helping individuals gain insights into their emotions, behaviors, and beliefs.

Fulfillment and Purpose: Holistic coaching assists individuals in discovering their life's purpose and finding a deeper sense of fulfillment.

The Significance of Holistic Coaching

Comprehensive Well-Being: Holistic coaching is significant for its focus on comprehensive well-being, addressing various aspects of an individual's life to foster personal growth and transformation.

Balance and Harmony: It plays a crucial role in helping individuals achieve balance and harmony in their lives, resulting in greater overall well-being.

Mind-Body-Spirit Connection: Holistic coaching acknowledges the importance of the mind-body-spirit connection and helps individuals explore their spiritual and emotional selves.

Sustainable Transformation: Holistic coaching supports sustainable transformation by fostering self-awareness, self-care practices, and personal growth.

Holistic coaching is a comprehensive and integrated approach to personal development and transformation that emphasizes the interconnectedness of various aspects of an individual's life.

By promoting self-awareness, emotional intelligence, and well-being in the physical, emotional, mental, and spiritual dimensions, it helps individuals achieve balance, harmony, and personal growth.

Holistic coaching is significant for its holistic well-being approach, its focus on balance and harmony, and its recognition of the mind-body-spirit connection, contributing to sustainable personal transformation and self-improvement.

Holistic Dental Hygiene: Nurturing Oral Health Naturally

Holistic dental hygiene is an approach to oral health that emphasizes the interconnectedness of oral well-being with overall physical and emotional health.

This holistic perspective goes beyond traditional dental care to encompass natural and sustainable practices that promote healthy teeth and gums. By recognizing the importance of a balanced, holistic approach, individuals can foster oral health that contributes to their overall well-being.

In this book, we will explore the principles, methods, benefits, and the significance of holistic dental hygiene, which encourages natural and holistic practices for maintaining a healthy and radiant smile.

Principles of Holistic Dental Hygiene

Interconnectedness: Holistic dental hygiene acknowledges the connection between oral health and overall physical and emotional well-being. It recognizes that oral health is not isolated but influences other aspects of health.

Natural and Non-Toxic: Holistic dental hygiene advocates for the use of natural and non-toxic oral care products, avoiding harmful chemicals, synthetic additives, and invasive treatments.

Nutritional Awareness: A balanced diet rich in vitamins and minerals is seen as essential for oral health, as well as overall well-being.

Preventive Care: Holistic dental hygiene emphasizes preventive care over reactive treatments, aiming to identify and address oral health issues at their root.

Methods and Techniques of Holistic Dental Hygiene

Natural Oral Care Products: Holistic dental hygiene promotes the use of natural toothpaste, mouthwash, and dental floss, avoiding ingredients like artificial colors and synthetic preservatives.

Nutrient-Rich Diet: A diet rich in essential nutrients, such as calcium, vitamin D, and vitamin C, is crucial for strong teeth and healthy gums.

Oil Pulling: Oil pulling with natural oils like coconut or sesame is believed to help remove toxins, reduce bacteria, and improve oral health.

Herbal Remedies: Holistic dental hygiene incorporates herbal remedies, like calendula or chamomile, for oral health support.

Mindful Eating: Chewing slowly and mindfully can improve digestion and oral health by promoting proper saliva production.

Benefits of Holistic Dental Hygiene

Improved Oral Health: Holistic dental hygiene can lead to healthier teeth and gums, reducing the risk of issues like cavities and gum disease.

Reduced Toxins: Avoiding harmful chemicals and using natural products can minimize the toxins entering your body.

Enhanced Overall Well-Being: By promoting a balanced diet and mindful eating, holistic dental hygiene contributes to better physical and emotional well-being.

Preventive Approach: This approach helps identify oral health issues early, preventing more severe problems in the future.

Eco-Friendly: Holistic dental hygiene supports eco-friendly and sustainable oral care practices, reducing waste and environmental impact.

The Significance of Holistic Dental Hygiene

Comprehensive Health: Holistic dental hygiene is significant for recognizing that oral health is interconnected with overall health and well-being. Non-Toxic Approach: By promoting the use of non-toxic and natural products, holistic dental hygiene minimizes the exposure to harmful chemicals.

Preventive Care: Emphasizing preventive care can help individuals avoid painful and costly dental procedures in the future.

Sustainable Practices: Holistic dental hygiene encourages sustainable and eco-friendly oral care practices, reducing the impact on the environment.

Holistic dental hygiene is an approach to oral health that promotes interconnectedness between oral well-being and overall physical and emotional health. By embracing natural and non-toxic oral care products, maintaining a nutrient-rich diet, and practicing preventive care, individuals can achieve a healthy and radiant smile. Holistic dental hygiene is significant for its holistic perspective, non-toxic approach, preventive care, and commitment to sustainable oral care practices, which contribute to both oral health and overall well-being.

Holistic Energy Psychology: A Comprehensive Approach to Holistic Healing

Holistic energy psychology is an integrative approach to holistic healing that combines energy psychology techniques with a broader perspective on well-being. It emphasizes the interconnectedness of emotional, mental, physical, and spiritual health and recognizes the role of energy in our overall well-being.

This holistic perspective goes beyond traditional healing methods to incorporate energy-based approaches that aim to balance and harmonize an individual's energy systems. In this book, we will explore the principles, methods, benefits, and significance of holistic energy psychology, which plays a vital role in achieving comprehensive holistic health and personal transformation.

Principles of Holistic Energy Psychology

Interconnectedness: Holistic energy psychology is based on the principle that emotional, mental, physical, and spiritual well-being are interconnected. It recognizes that imbalances in one area can affect others.

Energy Systems: It acknowledges the existence of energy systems within the body, such as chakras and meridians, and their impact on overall health.

Mind-Body-Spirit Alignment: Holistic energy psychology promotes the alignment of the mind, body, and spirit to achieve balance, harmony, and holistic well-being.

Personal Growth: It emphasizes personal growth and transformation through the release of energy blocks and emotional healing.

Methods and Techniques of Holistic Energy Psychology

Emotional Freedom Techniques (EFT): EFT, or "tapping," is a widely used technique that combines affirmations with acupressure to release emotional energy blockages.

Reiki: Reiki is a form of energy healing that uses the practitioner's hands to channel universal life force energy to the client, promoting relaxation and balance.

Chakra Balancing: Holistic energy psychology often includes chakra balancing, which involves using meditation, visualization, and energy work to align and clear the body's energy centers.

Energy Medicine: Energy medicine techniques, like Quantum Touch or Pranic Healing, aim to clear and balance the body's energy fields for improved health and well-being.

Guided Visualization: Holistic energy psychology incorporates guided visualization exercises to help individuals release emotional blocks and promote self-healing.

Benefits of Holistic Energy Psychology

Emotional Healing: Holistic energy psychology assists in the release of emotional traumas and energy blockages, promoting emotional healing and well-being.

Stress Reduction: Techniques like EFT and energy balancing can help reduce stress and promote relaxation, contributing to better mental and emotional health.

Improved Physical Health: By addressing energy imbalances, individuals may experience improved physical health, reduced pain, and enhanced vitality.

Personal Growth: Holistic energy psychology fosters personal growth and transformation by aligning the mind, body, and spirit.

Spiritual Connection: It enhances spiritual awareness and connection, promoting a deeper sense of purpose and self-awareness.

The Significance of Holistic Energy Psychology

Comprehensive Healing: Holistic energy psychology plays a significant role in comprehensive healing by addressing emotional, mental, physical, and spiritual aspects of an individual's well-being.

Balance and Harmony: It helps individuals achieve balance and harmony in their energy systems, fostering holistic well-being.

Emotional Healing: By releasing emotional traumas and energy blockages, it contributes to emotional healing and personal transformation.

Mind-Body-Spirit Alignment: Holistic energy psychology promotes the alignment of the mind, body, and spirit, fostering self-awareness and overall well-being.

Holistic energy psychology is an integrative approach to holistic healing that focuses on the interconnectedness of emotional, mental, physical, and spiritual well-being.

By combining energy psychology techniques with a holistic perspective, individuals can release emotional traumas, balance their energy systems, reduce stress, and promote personal growth and transformation. Holistic energy psychology is significant for its comprehensive healing approach, emphasis on balance and harmony, and role in emotional healing and personal transformation. It is a powerful tool for achieving holistic health and well-being.

Holistic Financial Coaching Services: Aligning Your Financial Practices with Holistic Values and Goals

Holistic financial coaching services are a comprehensive approach to financial planning and management that emphasizes the interconnectedness of financial well-being with overall physical, emotional, and spiritual health.

This holistic perspective goes beyond traditional financial advice to incorporate mindfulness, sustainable practices, and ethical investment strategies. Holistic financial coaching aims to guide individuals in aligning their financial practices with their core values and life goals, fostering financial well-being that complements their overall holistic health.

In this book, we will explore the principles, methods, benefits, and the significance of holistic financial coaching, which empowers individuals to create a financial plan that supports their holistic values and goals.

Principles of Holistic Financial Coaching

Interconnectedness: Holistic financial coaching is based on the principle that financial well-being is intertwined with physical, emotional, and spiritual health. It recognizes that financial decisions can impact other aspects of well-being.

Holistic Values: It promotes the alignment of financial practices with an individual's holistic values, which may include environmental sustainability, ethical investment, and social responsibility.

Mindful Money Management: Holistic financial coaching encourages mindful money management, which involves self-awareness, conscious spending, and ethical financial decisions.

Sustainable Wealth: It emphasizes the creation of sustainable wealth that supports long-term financial well-being and a positive impact on the world.

Methods and Techniques of Holistic Financial Coaching

Financial Assessment: Holistic financial coaching typically starts with a comprehensive financial assessment to understand an individual's current financial situation, goals, and values.

Mindful Budgeting: Mindful budgeting techniques, such as tracking spending, are used to promote self-awareness and conscious spending.

Ethical Investing: Holistic financial coaching includes guidance on ethical and sustainable investing that aligns with an individual's values and goals.

Sustainable Financial Practices: Coaching encourages sustainable financial practices, such as minimizing debt, reducing waste, and supporting ethical businesses.

Financial Mindfulness: Techniques like meditation and mindfulness are employed to help individuals develop a positive relationship with money and make conscious financial decisions.

Benefits of Holistic Financial Coaching

Financial Well-Being: Holistic financial coaching fosters financial well-being that aligns with an individual's holistic values and life goals.

Sustainable Wealth: It supports the creation of sustainable wealth that promotes long-term financial stability and ethical practices.

Personal Growth: Holistic financial coaching can lead to personal growth by enhancing self-awareness, ethical decision-making, and a mindful approach to money management.

Ethical Investments: Individuals can align their investments with their values, supporting businesses and initiatives that make a positive impact on society and the environment.

Mindful Financial Practices: Coaching encourages mindful spending, debt reduction, and ethical financial practices that reduce stress and promote well-being.

The Significance of Holistic Financial Coaching

Comprehensive Financial Well-Being: Holistic financial coaching is significant for its comprehensive approach to financial well-being that considers physical, emotional, and spiritual health.

Ethical Alignment: It promotes the alignment of financial practices with holistic values, allowing individuals to make ethical and sustainable financial decisions.

Sustainable Wealth: Holistic financial coaching plays a crucial role in creating sustainable wealth that supports long-term financial stability and ethical practices.

Mindful Money Management: By fostering mindful money management, it helps individuals make conscious financial decisions that reduce stress and contribute to their well-being.

Holistic financial coaching services offer a comprehensive approach to financial planning and management that aligns financial practices with an individual's holistic values and goals. By emphasizing interconnectedness, ethical financial decisions, mindful money management, and the creation of sustainable wealth, individuals can achieve financial well-being that complements their overall holistic health. Holistic financial coaching is significant for its holistic approach, ethical alignment, emphasis on sustainable wealth, and support for mindful money management, ultimately contributing to the well-being of both the individual and the world.

Holistic Financial Planning: Aligning Your Finances with Holistic Values and Goals

Holistic financial planning is an all-encompassing approach to managing your financial well-being that goes beyond traditional financial strategies.

It emphasizes the interconnectedness of your financial health with your overall physical, emotional, and spiritual well-being.

Holistic financial planning recognizes that your financial decisions have a significant impact on other areas of your life. By aligning your finances with your holistic values and life goals, you can achieve not only monetary success but also overall well-being.

In this book, we will explore the principles, methods, benefits, and the significance of holistic financial planning, which empowers individuals to create a financial plan that supports their holistic values and goals.

Principles of Holistic Financial Planning

Interconnectedness: Holistic financial planning is based on the principle that financial well-being is deeply intertwined with physical, emotional, and spiritual health. It acknowledges that financial decisions can have far-reaching consequences.

Holistic Values: It promotes the alignment of financial practices with an individual's holistic values, which may include ethical investments, sustainable living, and social responsibility.

Mindful Money Management: Holistic financial planning encourages mindful money management, involving self-awareness, responsible spending, and ethical financial choices.

Sustainable Wealth: This approach aims to create sustainable wealth that not only benefits the individual but also has a positive impact on the world.

Methods and Techniques of Holistic Financial Planning

Financial Assessment: Holistic financial planning often begins with a comprehensive financial assessment. This assessment helps you understand your current financial situation, your goals, and how they align with your values.

Mindful Budgeting: Mindful budgeting techniques, such as tracking spending, are used to promote self-awareness and responsible financial practices.

Ethical Investments: Holistic financial planning provides guidance on ethical and sustainable investing. This allows you to invest in companies and initiatives that align with your values and goals.

Sustainable Financial Practices: You are encouraged to adopt sustainable financial practices like reducing debt, minimizing waste, and supporting ethical businesses.

Financial Mindfulness: Techniques such as meditation and mindfulness are employed to help you develop a healthy relationship with money and make conscious financial decisions.

Benefits of Holistic Financial Planning

Financial Well-Being: Holistic financial planning fosters financial well-being that aligns with your holistic values and life goals.

Sustainable Wealth: It supports the creation of sustainable wealth, which promotes long-term financial stability and ethical practices.

Personal Growth: Holistic financial planning can lead to personal growth by enhancing self-awareness, ethical decision-making, and a mindful approach to money management.

Ethical Investments: You can align your investments with your values, supporting businesses and initiatives that make a positive impact on society and the environment.

Mindful Financial Practices: Holistic financial planning encourages mindful spending, debt reduction, and ethical financial practices that reduce stress and promote well-being.

The Significance of Holistic Financial Planning

Comprehensive Financial Well-Being: Holistic financial planning is significant for its comprehensive approach to financial well-being, considering physical, emotional, and spiritual health.

Ethical Alignment: It promotes the alignment of financial practices with holistic values, enabling individuals to make ethical and sustainable financial decisions.

Sustainable Wealth: Holistic financial planning plays a crucial role in creating sustainable wealth that supports long-term financial stability and ethical practices.

Mindful Money Management: By fostering mindful money management, it helps individuals make conscious financial decisions that reduce stress and contribute to overall well-being.

Holistic financial planning offers a comprehensive approach to managing your financial well-being. By emphasizing interconnectedness, ethical financial decisions, mindful money management, and the creation of sustainable wealth, individuals can achieve financial well-being that complements their overall holistic health. Holistic financial planning is significant for its holistic approach, ethical alignment, emphasis on sustainable wealth, and support for mindful money management, ultimately contributing to the well-being of both the individual and the world.

Holistic Health Advancements: The Evolution of Holistic Well-Being Practices

Holistic health is an approach to well-being that considers the interconnectedness of physical, emotional, mental, and spiritual aspects of an individual's life. Over the years, holistic health practices have evolved significantly, reflecting a growing understanding of how all aspects of our lives contribute to overall health. From ancient healing traditions to cutting-edge innovations, this book explores the advancements in holistic health practices that have contributed to the development of a more comprehensive and integrated approach to well-being.

Ancient Wisdom and Holistic Health

Holistic health has deep roots in ancient healing traditions from around the world. These practices laid the foundation for the modern holistic approach. Some notable examples include:

Traditional Chinese Medicine (TCM): TCM emphasizes the balance of qi (energy) and the harmonious functioning of the body's organ systems. Acupuncture, herbal medicine, and qigong are integral to TCM.

Ayurveda: Originating in India, Ayurveda focuses on balancing the three doshas (Vata, Pitta, and Kapha) to maintain health. It incorporates herbal remedies, diet, and yoga.

Native American Healing: Indigenous healing practices emphasize the connection between individuals and the natural world. Rituals, herbs, and energy work are common components of Native American holistic health.

Yoga and Meditation: Practices like yoga and meditation have ancient origins and are now widely recognized for promoting physical and emotional well-being.

Modern Advancements in Holistic Health

In recent decades, holistic health practices have evolved, incorporating new knowledge, research, and technology. Here are some modern advancements:

Integrative Medicine: Integrative medicine combines conventional and complementary approaches to health. It includes therapies such as chiropractic care, naturopathy, and integrative nutrition.

Functional Medicine: Functional medicine identifies and addresses the root causes of diseases, focusing on personalized treatments, diet, lifestyle, and genetic factors.

Mind-Body Therapies: Techniques like Mindfulness-Based Stress Reduction (MBSR) and Cognitive Behavioral Therapy (CBT) have gained popularity for their effectiveness in reducing stress, managing chronic illnesses, and improving mental health.

Energy Healing: Energy healing practices, like Reiki and Healing Touch, work to balance the body's energy systems to promote healing and well-being.

Nutrigenomics: This field explores how an individual's genetics affect their dietary needs, leading to more personalized nutrition and health plans.

Holistic Health in Mainstream Medicine

One significant advancement in holistic health is its increasing acceptance in mainstream medicine.

Medical institutions and professionals are recognizing the benefits of a holistic approach. Some noteworthy developments include:

Mindfulness in Healthcare: Mindfulness practices are incorporated into clinical settings to reduce stress, anxiety, and depression in patients.

Lifestyle Medicine: Medical professionals are focusing on lifestyle factors, such as diet, exercise, and stress management, as primary interventions or chronic diseases.

Holistic Nursing: Holistic nursing recognizes the importance of caring for patients' physical, emotional, and spiritual needs, contributing to more patient-centered care.

Mind-Body Medicine: The integration of mind-body techniques, such as guided imagery and relaxation exercises, helps patients manage pain, improve sleep, and enhance overall well-being.

Holistic Education: Medical schools and nursing programs increasingly include holistic approaches in their curricula, ensuring that healthcare professionals are trained in holistic care.

Technological Innovations

Advancements in technology have also played a significant role in the evolution of holistic health:

Health and Wellness Apps: Mobile apps provide guided meditation, exercise routines, nutrition tracking, and stress management tools, making holistic practices more accessible.

Wearable Health Devices: Devices like fitness trackers and smartwatches monitor physical activity, sleep, and stress levels, helping individuals make informed decisions about their health.

Telemedicine: Virtual healthcare consultations offer convenient access to holistic practitioners, enabling people to receive personalized care from the comfort of their homes.

Biofeedback and Neurofeedback: These technologies help individuals gain awareness and control over their physiological responses, assisting in stress management and overall well-being.

Significance of Holistic Health Advancements

The advancements in holistic health practices are significant for several reasons:

Holistic Approach: These advancements promote a more comprehensive approach to health, recognizing that emotional, mental, and spiritual factors are equally important as physical health.

Personalization: Advances like functional medicine, nutrigenomics, and lifestyle medicine allow for personalized care and treatment plans that cater to an individual's unique needs and preferences.

Integration: The integration of holistic health practices into mainstream medicine ensures that patients receive a more well-rounded approach to their healthcare.

Accessibility: Technological innovations make holistic practices more accessible to a wider audience, allowing individuals to take charge of their well-being.

Holistic health has evolved significantly from its ancient roots, integrating modern science, technology, and a deeper understanding of the interconnectedness of well-being.

Holistic Health Innovations: Pioneering a New Era of Well-Being

Holistic health is an approach to well-being that recognizes the interconnectedness of physical, emotional, mental, and spiritual health. Over the years, holistic health practices have undergone significant innovation, expanding and evolving to meet the diverse needs of individuals seeking comprehensive well-being. In this book, we will explore the latest holistic health innovations, highlighting groundbreaking advancements that contribute to a more integrative and personalized approach to health and wellness.

Personalized Nutrition and Nutrigenomics:

Nutrigenomics is an emerging field that studies how an individual's genes interact with their diet. It provides insights into how our unique genetic makeup influences our dietary needs. Advances in personalized nutrition use this information to create individualized dietary plans, optimizing nutrient intake and reducing the risk of nutrition-related diseases. These personalized plans consider genetic factors, dietary preferences, and health goals.

Digital Health and Wellness Platforms:

Digital health platforms and wellness apps have revolutionized holistic health by offering convenient tools for tracking and managing well-being. These platforms provide features like fitness and sleep tracking, guided meditation, stress management exercises, and nutrition planning. They enable individuals to access holistic health practices and guidance from the comfort of their smartphones or other devices.

Mindfulness and Meditation Apps:

Mindfulness and meditation have gained widespread recognition for their positive impact on mental and emotional well-being. There are now numerous apps that offer guided meditation sessions, mindfulness practices, and stress reduction techniques. These apps make it easy for individuals to incorporate these practices into their daily routines, enhancing their emotional and mental health.

Telehealth and Virtual Holistic Consultations:

Telehealth has become a prominent innovation, especially in the wake of the COVID-19 pandemic. It offers the ability to access holistic practitioners remotely through virtual consultations. This advancement provides greater accessibility to holistic care, ensuring that individuals can receive personalized guidance and support from experienced professionals without the need for in-person visits.

Advanced Energy Healing Modalities:

Energy healing practices, such as Reiki and Healing Touch, continue to evolve with new techniques and approaches. These practices aim to balance and harmonize an individual's energy systems, promoting healing and well-being. Innovations in this field involve the integration of technology and energy work, allowing practitioners to fine-tune their methods and provide more effective treatments.

Integrative Wellness Centers:

Integrative wellness centers are emerging as comprehensive hubs for holistic well-being. They combine various holistic practices, including yoga, meditation, acupuncture, and massage therapy, under one roof. These centers create a one-stop destination for individuals seeking diverse holistic health experiences and support.

Biofeedback and Neurofeedback:

Biofeedback and neurofeedback technologies are gaining prominence for their ability to provide real-time data on physiological responses. These technologies help individuals gain awareness and control over their stress levels, heart rate, brainwave activity, and more. They are used in stress management and emotional well-being practices, enhancing the effectiveness of holistic health treatments.

Genetic and Epigenetic Testing for Well-Being:

Genetic testing for health and well-being has expanded to include insights into an individual's predisposition to certain conditions, optimal exercise routines, and nutritional needs. Epigenetic testing, which analyzes how lifestyle choices affect gene expression, provides further guidance on optimizing well-being. These innovative approaches empower individuals to make personalized health decisions based on their genetic makeup.

Significance of Holistic Health Innovations

The significance of these holistic health innovations lies in their ability to:

Enhance Personalization: Innovations such as nutrigenomics, genetic testing, and epigenetic analysis allow for more personalized approaches to well-being, considering individual variations in health needs and goals.

Improve Accessibility: Digital health platforms, virtual consultations, and wellness apps make holistic health practices and guidance more accessible to a broader audience, breaking down geographical barriers.

Optimize Holistic Practices: Integrating technology with holistic practices enhances the effectiveness of these treatments, enabling individuals to experience more significant benefits.

 Promote Holistic Well-Being: These innovations support the holistic well-being of individuals by addressing physical, emotional, mental, and spiritual aspects of health in a comprehensive and interconnected manner.

Holistic health innovations continue to push the boundaries of well-being, offering new ways to address physical, emotional, mental, and spiritual health in an interconnected manner. These advancements promote personalization, accessibility, and the optimization of holistic practices, ultimately contributing to a more holistic and comprehensive approach to well-being. As holistic health continues to evolve, it is poised to offer even more advanced and effective ways to support the health and well-being of individuals worldwide.

Holistic Life Design: Crafting a Life Aligned with Your Holistic Values and Aspirations

Holistic life design is an intentional and integrated approach to creating a life that aligns with your deepest values, aspirations, and well-being. It recognizes that well-being extends beyond physical health and encompasses emotional, mental, and spiritual dimensions. This book explores the principles, methods, and significance of holistic life design, offering a framework to help individuals structure their lives in a way that reflects their unique holistic values and goals.

Principles of Holistic Life Design

Interconnectedness: Holistic life design is founded on the belief that all aspects of life are interconnected. It acknowledges that decisions and choices in one area of life impact other facets, whether physical, emotional, mental, or spiritual.

Holistic Values: It emphasizes the importance of identifying your holistic values, such as sustainability, mindfulness, social responsibility, and balance. These values guide your choices and actions in all areas of life.

Purpose and Vision: Holistic life design encourages you to develop a clear purpose and vision for your life. These act as guiding lights, helping you align your actions and decisions with your aspirations.

Well-Being-Centric: Well-being takes center stage in holistic life design. It prioritizes physical health, emotional balance, mental clarity, and spiritual growth to create a well-rounded, flourishing life.

Methods and Techniques of Holistic Life Design

Self-Reflection and Awareness: Start by examining your current life and well-being. What are your holistic values, and how well are you living in alignment with them? Regular self-reflection and self-awareness are foundational practices in holistic life design.

Goal Setting: Define specific, holistic goals that reflect your values and aspirations. These goals can encompass physical health, emotional well-being, personal growth, career aspirations, or anything that resonates with your holistic vision.

Intentional Time Management: Manage your time in a way that honors your holistic values and goals. Prioritize activities and commitments that align with your vision and minimize those that detract from it.

Mindful Decision-Making: Make conscious, mindful decisions in all areas of your life, considering how each choice impacts your holistic well-being. Whether it's related to career, relationships, or personal development, ensure that your choices resonate with your values.

Balanced Lifestyle: Achieving balance is a core tenet of holistic life design. Balance your work, leisure, relationships, and self-care to support well-being in all dimensions of your life.

Benefits of Holistic Life Design

Authenticity: Holistic life design encourages you to live authentically, in alignment with your true self and deepest values.

Enhanced Well-Being: By focusing on well-being in its various dimensions, you can experience greater physical health, emotional balance, mental clarity, and spiritual fulfillment.

Clarity and Purpose: Having a clear purpose and vision for your life provides a sense of direction and meaning, helping you stay motivated and focused.

Resilience: When you live in alignment with your values, you become more resilient in the face of challenges and setbacks.

Greater Fulfillment: Structuring your life according to your holistic values and goals often leads to a greater sense of fulfillment and contentment.

The Significance of Holistic Life Design

Comprehensive Well-Being: Holistic life design is significant for its comprehensive approach to well-being. It addresses all facets of your life and provides a roadmap for thriving in each dimension.

Alignment with Values: It enables individuals to live in alignment with their core values, fostering authenticity and purpose in their lives.

Resilience: A life designed holistically equips individuals with greater resilience and adaptability, enabling them to navigate life's challenges with grace.

Fulfillment: Holistic life design significantly contributes to personal fulfillment, as it encourages individuals to live in accordance with their passions and aspirations.

Holistic life design is a purposeful and integrative approach to crafting a life that aligns with your values and well-being. By embracing the interconnectedness of all aspects of life, setting holistic goals, and living in alignment with your core values, you can create a life that reflects your deepest aspirations and values.

Holistic life design is significant for its comprehensive approach, alignment with values, resilience-building, and the potential for personal fulfillment. It offers a powerful framework for structuring your life in a way that honors your holistic well-being.

Holistic Marketing: Promoting Businesses and Services with Ethical and Holistic Values

Holistic marketing is a multifaceted approach to promoting businesses and services that extends beyond traditional marketing strategies. It emphasizes the interconnectedness of all elements of marketing, including the products or services, the well-being of consumers, and the impact on society and the environment. This approach is rooted in ethical values, sustainability, and a commitment to the well-being of all stakeholders. In this book, we will explore the principles, methods, benefits, and significance of holistic marketing, which aims to create a more ethical, sustainable, and socially responsible business environment.

Principles of Holistic Marketing

Interconnectedness: Holistic marketing recognizes the interdependence of different aspects of marketing, including product design, promotion, pricing, and distribution. It acknowledges that all these elements impact each other and that they collectively influence the well-being of consumers and the environment.

Ethical Values: It is rooted in ethical values and principles. Holistic marketing aims to ensure that business practices are aligned with moral standards and the well-being of society.

Sustainability: Sustainability is a core principle of holistic marketing. It seeks to create marketing strategies that do not deplete natural resources, harm the environment, or negatively impact future generations.

Consumer Well-Being: Holistic marketing prioritizes the well-being of consumers by providing products and services that contribute positively to their health, happiness, and overall quality of life.

Methods and Techniques of Holistic Marketing

Ethical Product Development: Holistic marketing begins with the design of products or services that are ethical and contribute to the well-being of consumers. For example, organic and environmentally friendly products are promoted over those that are harmful to health or the environment.

Sustainability Practices: Holistic marketing incorporates sustainable practices in the supply chain and manufacturing processes. This includes responsible sourcing, waste reduction, and energy-efficient production.

Customer Education: Businesses using holistic marketing educate customers about the ethical and sustainable aspects of their products. This empowers consumers to make informed choices aligned with their values.

Social Responsibility: Holistic marketing often includes initiatives to give back to the community or support social and environmental causes. Businesses may donate a portion of their profits, engage in volunteer work, or support sustainable projects.

Transparency: Transparent communication is vital in holistic marketing. Businesses are open and honest about their practices, sourcing, and the impact of their products on health and the environment.

Benefits of Holistic Marketing

Enhanced Reputation: Holistic marketing builds a positive reputation for businesses, enhancing their credibility and trustworthiness among consumers.

Loyal Customer Base: Consumers who value ethical and sustainable products are more likely to become loyal customers of businesses practicing holistic marketing.

Competitive Advantage: Holistic marketing provides a competitive edge by appealing to the growing market of environmentally conscious and ethically minded consumers.

Sustainability: Businesses adopting holistic marketing practices contribute to sustainability, which benefits the planet and future generations.

Consumer Well-Being: Holistic marketing promotes products and services that improve the health and well-being of consumers, fostering happier and more satisfied customers.

The Significance of Holistic Marketing

Ethical and Sustainable Business Practices: Holistic marketing plays a significant role in promoting ethical and sustainable business practices, which are essential for a healthier and more responsible global economy.

Well-Being-Focused: It prioritizes the well-being of consumers, emphasizing the importance of providing products and services that contribute to their health and happiness.

Social Responsibility: Holistic marketing highlights the importance of businesses giving back to society and supporting causes that make a positive impact.

Consumer-Centric Approach: This approach is consumer-centric, focusing on meeting the needs and values of consumers, which is increasingly important in today's market.

Holistic marketing is a comprehensive approach to promoting businesses and services that prioritizes ethical values, sustainability, and the well-being of consumers.

By emphasizing interconnectedness, ethical product development, sustainability practices, consumer education, social responsibility, and transparency, businesses can build positive reputations, loyal customer bases, and competitive advantages.

Holistic marketing is significant for promoting ethical and sustainable business practices, consumer well-being, social responsibility, and a consumer-centric approach to marketing. It contributes to a more ethical, sustainable, and socially responsible business environment.

Holistic Music Composition: Creating Harmonious Sounds for Healing and Relaxation

Holistic music composition is an approach to creating music that aims to promote healing, relaxation, and overall well-being. It recognizes the profound connection between music, emotions, and the human spirit. Through a combination of carefully chosen elements like tempo, instrumentation, and harmony, holistic music composition seeks to create an auditory experience that nurtures the mind, body, and soul. In this book, we will explore the principles, methods, benefits, and significance of holistic music composition in promoting healing and relaxation.

Principles of Holistic Music Composition

Interconnectedness: Holistic music composition acknowledges the interconnectedness of human emotions, physical sensations, and spiritual experiences. Music is seen as a means to harmonize and balance these dimensions.

Mindful Intent: Composers focus on creating music with the mindful intent of fostering relaxation, healing, and emotional well-being. The music's purpose is to serve the listener's holistic health.

Emotionally Intelligent: Holistic music is emotionally intelligent, understanding how different musical elements can evoke specific emotional responses, such as calmness, happiness, or introspection.

Resonance with Nature: It draws inspiration from the natural world, as the rhythms, tones, and melodies are often designed to resonate with the natural rhythms and patterns found in nature.

Methods and Techniques of Holistic Music Composition

Tone and Melody: Holistic composers pay close attention to the choice of tones and melodies, selecting those that evoke feelings of serenity, joy, and emotional release.

Instrumentation: The selection of instruments plays a crucial role in holistic music composition. Composers often use soft, gentle, and natural sounds like flutes, acoustic guitars, and harps.

Rhythms and Tempo: Holistic music often features slow and steady rhythms, mirroring the natural flow of breath and heart rate. This steady tempo induces a sense of relaxation.

Harmony and Balance: Composers aim for harmonic balance, creating a sense of completeness and unity that can promote a feeling of inner peace.

Nature Sounds: Many holistic compositions incorporate sounds from nature, such as flowing water, birdsong, or rustling leaves. These elements connect the listener with the natural world.

Benefits of Holistic Music Composition

Stress Reduction: Holistic music is well-known for its stress-reducing effects. It can lower cortisol levels, promote relaxation, and reduce the physical and emotional effects of stress.

Emotional Release: The emotionally intelligent design of holistic music allows listeners to release and process emotions, leading to a sense of emotional well-being.

Improved Sleep: Holistic compositions can promote better sleep quality by calming the mind and helping individuals transition into a restful state.

Enhanced Mindfulness: The mindful intent behind holistic music can encourage mindfulness and presence, helping individuals become more attuned to the present moment.

Emotional Healing: The healing power of music can assist individuals in coping with trauma, grief, and emotional pain, providing solace and support.

The Significance of Holistic Music Composition

Emotional and Mental Health: Holistic music plays a significant role in promoting emotional and mental health by offering a therapeutic and expressive outlet for individuals.

Stress Reduction: In an increasingly stressful world, holistic music serves as a valuable tool for reducing stress and anxiety, contributing to overall well-being.

Healing and Recovery: Holistic music can be an essential part of the healing and recovery process, aiding individuals in their journey to emotional and physical well-being.

Emotional Expression: It offers a medium for emotional expression and processing, allowing individuals to connect with their inner feelings and experiences.

Holistic music composition is a thoughtful and intentional approach to creating music that fosters relaxation, healing, and emotional well-being.

By emphasizing interconnectedness, mindful intent, emotional intelligence, and resonance with nature, holistic music composers create harmonious sounds that promote holistic health. Holistic music is significant for its role in supporting emotional and mental health, reducing stress, aiding in healing and recovery, and offering a channel for emotional expression.

In a world where well-being is increasingly important, holistic music serves as a valuable tool for promoting relaxation and healing.

Holistic Music Festivals: Harmonizing Mind, Body, and Spirit Through Healing Sounds

Music has the power to evoke powerful emotions and affect our overall well-being. Holistic music festivals, a relatively recent addition to the festival landscape, focus on harnessing this power for the betterment of the mind, body, and spirit. These unique events prioritize music that promotes healing, relaxation, and personal growth, offering attendees an immersive experience like no other. In this book, we will explore the world of holistic music festivals, their underlying principles, and the benefits they offer.

The Essence of Holistic Music Festivals

The Holistic Approach

Holistic music festivals are built on the principles of holistic wellness. They consider the interconnectedness of the mind, body, and spirit and aim to harmonize these elements through music. The music selection is carefully curated to provide a multisensory experience, often blending genres like ambient, world music, jazz, and classical, along with live sound healing sessions.

Healing Sounds

A key element of holistic music festivals is the use of music as a therapeutic tool. The selected music often incorporates soothing melodies, nature-inspired sounds, and frequencies believed to have healing properties. Sound healing techniques, such as crystal singing bowl sessions and gong baths, are frequently featured to facilitate relaxation and inner balance.

Benefits of Holistic Music Festivals

Stress Reduction

Holistic music festivals offer attendees an opportunity to escape from the stresses of daily life. The calming sounds and tranquil atmosphere can lead to reduced stress levels, ultimately promoting relaxation and mental well-being.

Mindfulness and Meditation

Music at these festivals encourages mindfulness and meditation. As the soothing sounds envelop the audience, it becomes easier to focus on the present moment, enhancing the meditative experience. Guided meditation sessions are often part of the festival's program.

Enhanced Emotional Well-being

The emotive power of music is harnessed to promote emotional healing and self-discovery. Attendees often report experiencing a range of emotions, from deep introspection to joy and elation. This emotional journey can lead to greater self-awareness and personal growth.

Improved Physical Health

The healing properties of music are believed to have a positive impact on physical health. Sound healing modalities like binaural beats and Solfeggio frequencies are thought to stimulate cellular repair and promote physical healing.

Connection and Community

Holistic music festivals create a sense of community among like-minded individuals. The shared experience of music and healing can lead to lasting connections, making these festivals an excellent place to meet people who share a passion for holistic wellness.

Key Elements of Holistic Music Festivals

Music Selection

The music at these festivals is curated with care, selecting genres and artists known for their ability to create a relaxing and healing atmosphere. Some festivals also include workshops on how to use music as a self-care tool.

Sound Healing Sessions

Sound healing sessions are integral to holistic festivals. These sessions often involve instruments like crystal singing bowls, Tibetan singing bowls, gongs, and tuning forks, which are believed to help realign the body's energy and promote healing.

Yoga and Movement

Holistic festivals frequently feature yoga and movement classes to complement the healing power of music. Attendees can participate in various classes to enhance their physical and mental well-being.

Workshops and Talks

Workshops and talks on subjects like meditation, mindfulness, energy healing, and the science of sound are common features. These educational sessions provide valuable information and tools for personal growth and holistic living.

Notable Holistic Music Festivals

Wanderlust Festival

Wanderlust is a renowned holistic music festival that combines yoga, mindfulness, and wellness with live music. It is held in various locations worldwide and attracts a diverse audience seeking a holistic festival experience.

Envision Festival

Envision Festival, located in Costa Rica, is an eco-conscious event that blends world music, art, and yoga, creating a vibrant space for personal and collective transformation.

BaliSpirit Festival

BaliSpirit Festival in Indonesia offers a unique blend of music, movement, and healing arts. It celebrates the rich cultural and spiritual traditions of Bali, making it an immersive experience for attendees.

Holistic music festivals represent a unique and powerful convergence of music, wellness, and spirituality.

These events provide a space for individuals to escape the chaos of daily life, connect with like-minded individuals, and embark on a journey of self-discovery and healing.

The healing power of music, combined with sound healing sessions, meditation, and educational workshops, makes holistic music festivals a compelling avenue for those seeking to enhance their overall well-being and find balance in the modern world.

Holistic Nutrition Certification Programs: Paving the Path to Nutritional Wellness

In today's world, the emphasis on holistic well-being and nutrition has grown significantly. People are increasingly looking for personalized, natural, and sustainable approaches to health, which has led to the rise of holistic nutrition practices. Holistic nutrition certification programs have gained prominence, offering individuals the knowledge and skills to understand and advocate for a holistic approach to nutrition. In this book, we will explore the world of holistic nutrition certification programs, their core principles, and the professional benefits they offer.

The Essence of Holistic Nutrition

Holistic Approach to Nutrition

Holistic nutrition is based on the concept that health is influenced by a myriad of factors beyond just the food we consume. It takes into account the interconnectedness of physical, emotional, mental, and spiritual well-being. A holistic nutritionist focuses on addressing the root causes of health issues, not just the symptoms, and aims to create customized nutrition plans to promote balance and vitality.

Whole Foods Emphasis

Holistic nutrition places a strong emphasis on whole, unprocessed, and nutrient-dense foods. It encourages individuals to choose foods that are as close to their natural state as possible, while minimizing the consumption of processed, artificial, and chemically laden foods.

Individualized Nutrition

One size does not fit all in holistic nutrition. Certified holistic nutritionists assess each client's unique needs, lifestyle, and goals to create tailored nutrition plans that promote optimal health. This approach recognizes that what works for one person may not work for another.

The Benefits of Holistic Nutrition Certification Programs

In-Depth Knowledge

Holistic nutrition certification programs provide a comprehensive education in nutrition, including biochemistry, physiology, and the role of nutrients in health. This knowledge equips practitioners to understand the intricate relationships between diet and well-being.

Holistic Assessment Skills

Graduates of these programs develop the ability to assess clients holistically, taking into account not only their dietary habits but also their emotional and mental well-being, lifestyle choices, and overall health status.

Personal and Professional Growth

Beyond nutrition, holistic nutrition programs often delve into personal growth and development, teaching skills like active listening, communication, and empathy. This personal development can significantly enhance a practitioner's ability to connect with clients on a deeper level.

Nutritional Counseling Skills

Certification programs equip students with the skills needed to provide one-on-one nutritional counseling, group workshops, and educational sessions. These practical skills are essential for helping individuals make positive dietary changes.

Career Opportunities

Graduates of holistic nutrition programs may pursue a variety of career paths, including working as holistic nutrition consultants, wellness coaches, or educators. They can also integrate their knowledge into existing healthcare practices, such as chiropractic care, naturopathy, or alternative medicine.

Core Components of Holistic Nutrition Certification Programs

Nutrition Science

Holistic nutrition programs include a strong foundation in nutrition science, covering topics like macronutrients, micronutrients, digestion, and the role of nutrients in the body.

Whole Food Nutrition

Emphasis is placed on the importance of whole, nutrient-dense foods and their positive impact on health. Students learn how to select and prepare these foods for maximum nutritional benefit.

Holistic Assessment

Students are trained to conduct holistic assessments of clients, considering physical, emotional, mental, and spiritual aspects of their well-being.

Therapeutic Diets

Holistic nutritionists learn to design therapeutic diets tailored to individual needs, which may include addressing food allergies, sensitivities, or specific health conditions.

Counseling and Communication

Communication skills are vital for understanding clients' needs, building rapport, and facilitating behavior change. Holistic nutrition programs often include coursework on effective counseling techniques.

Prominent Holistic Nutrition Certification Programs

Nutritional Therapy Association (NTA)

The NTA offers a Nutritional Therapy Practitioner (NTP) program that focuses on foundational principles of holistic nutrition, nutritional assessment, and personalized healing protocols.

Institute for Integrative Nutrition (IIN)

IIN offers a comprehensive Health Coach Training Program that covers various dietary theories, coaching skills, and holistic approaches to wellness.

Hawthorn University

Hawthorn University offers a Master of Science in Holistic Nutrition program that includes advanced courses in holistic nutrition, clinical skills, and research methods.

Holistic nutrition certification programs are instrumental in preparing individuals to promote overall well-being through a holistic approach to nutrition. These programs not only equip students with a deep understanding of nutrition science but also teach the importance of individualized care, whole foods, and the interconnectedness of physical, emotional, and mental health. Graduates of these programs play a vital role in helping individuals achieve optimal health and well-being through informed, holistic dietary choices.

Holistic Nutrition Coaching: Nourishing the Mind, Body, and Soul

Holistic nutrition coaching is a dynamic and evolving field that focuses on nurturing the mind, body, and soul through personalized dietary and lifestyle guidance. In an era where well-being encompasses more than just physical health, holistic nutrition coaches play a crucial role in helping individuals achieve comprehensive wellness. This book delves into the world of holistic nutrition coaching, explaining its principles, the benefits it offers, and the significance of seeking guidance from holistic nutrition coaches.

Understanding Holistic Nutrition Coaching

Holistic Approach

Holistic nutrition coaching is built on the fundamental principle that health is a product of the interplay between the physical, emotional, mental, and spiritual aspects of an individual's life.

It recognizes that nourishing the body with wholesome foods is just one part of a broader wellness picture.

Personalized Nutrition

Holistic nutrition coaches develop customized dietary and lifestyle plans for their clients. These plans consider the individual's unique needs, preferences, and goals, and they emphasize whole foods, mindful eating, and dietary choices that promote physical, emotional, and mental balance.

The Benefits of Holistic Nutrition Coaching

Comprehensive Wellness

Holistic nutrition coaching aims to enhance all aspects of a person's well-being, not just their physical health. It considers factors like emotional eating, stress management, sleep quality, and spirituality, helping clients achieve a more balanced and fulfilling life.

Personalized Approach

Unlike generic diets, holistic nutrition coaching recognizes that what works for one person may not work for another. Coaches work closely with clients to develop individualized nutrition plans that address specific health goals and challenges.

Mindful Eating

Holistic nutrition coaching promotes mindful eating, which encourages clients to be fully present and conscious of their food choices. This practice fosters a deeper connection with food, leading to healthier relationships with eating and a reduced risk of emotional eating.

Emotional Support

Holistic nutrition coaches often provide emotional support and guidance, helping clients address issues such as stress eating, emotional triggers, and other psychological aspects of nutrition. This support can be invaluable for long-term dietary changes.

Sustainable Lifestyle Changes

Holistic nutrition coaching focuses on cultivating sustainable habits that clients can maintain over the long term. This approach minimizes the risk of yo-yo dieting and supports lasting health improvements.

The Role of Holistic Nutrition Coaches

Assessment

Coaches assess clients' dietary habits, lifestyle choices, and overall health to understand their unique needs and challenges.

Education

Holistic nutrition coaches educate clients about the importance of whole foods, mindful eating, and the role of nutrition in overall wellness.

Customized Plans

Coaches create individualized nutrition plans tailored to each client's goals, which may include weight management, improving energy levels, managing chronic conditions, or emotional well-being.

Guidance and Support

Coaches offer ongoing support and guidance as clients work toward their goals, helping them overcome obstacles and make sustainable changes.

Empowerment

Holistic nutrition coaches empower clients to take charge of their health by providing the knowledge and tools needed to make informed, healthy choices.

Finding a Holistic Nutrition Coach

Certification

When seeking a holistic nutrition coach, it's essential to look for a certified professional. Organizations like the National Association of Nutrition Professionals (NANP) and the Nutritional Therapy Association (NTA) provide certification programs for holistic nutrition coaches.

Experience and Specialization

Consider a coach's experience and any specializations they may have. Some coaches focus on specific areas, such as digestive health, autoimmune conditions, or emotional eating.

Compatibility

Building a strong client-coach relationship is essential. Choose a coach with whom you feel comfortable and aligned in terms of goals and values.

Holistic nutrition coaching represents a powerful and comprehensive approach to achieving wellness.

By recognizing the interconnectedness of physical, emotional, mental, and spiritual well-being, holistic nutrition coaches play a pivotal role in helping individuals nourish not only their bodies but also their minds and souls.

The personalized approach and guidance offered by these coaches empower clients to make lasting, sustainable changes that lead to a more balanced and fulfilling life.

When seeking to improve your well-being, holistic nutrition coaching can be a valuable resource on your journey to holistic health.

Holistic Parenting Resources: Nurturing Mind, Body, and Soul

Holistic parenting represents an approach to child-rearing that considers the well-being of the child as a whole, taking into account not only their physical health but also their emotional, mental, and spiritual development. To assist parents in their holistic parenting journey, a wealth of resources and support is available. In this book, we will explore the world of holistic parenting resources, shedding light on the principles, benefits, and where to find guidance for parents interested in raising well-rounded, balanced children.

Holistic Parenting: An Overview

Holistic Philosophy

Holistic parenting is founded on the belief that children thrive when they are nurtured physically, emotionally, mentally, and spiritually. It recognizes the interconnectedness of these facets and their impact on a child's overall development.

Wholesome Nutrition

Proper nutrition is central to holistic parenting. It emphasizes whole foods, mindful eating, and a balanced diet to support a child's physical and mental growth. A holistic approach takes into account any dietary sensitivities or allergies and focuses on the importance of nutrient-dense foods.

Emotional Well-Being

Holistic parenting encourages emotional intelligence and healthy emotional expression. Parents are guided to create a supportive environment where children can process their feelings and develop coping mechanisms for life's challenges.

Mental and Intellectual Growth

Stimulating a child's intellectual curiosity and cognitive development is a key aspect of holistic parenting. This may involve reading, creative play, and educational activities that align with the child's age and interests.

Spiritual Development

Holistic parenting respects and supports a child's spiritual growth, allowing them to explore their beliefs and values. It encourages open-mindedness and acceptance of diverse spiritual and cultural perspectives.

The Benefits of Holistic Parenting

Well-Rounded Children

Holistic parenting aims to raise well-rounded children who are not only physically healthy but also emotionally stable, intellectually curious, and spiritually aware.

Healthy Lifestyle Habits

By instilling a love for wholesome foods and an appreciation for physical activity, holistic parenting encourages the development of healthy lifestyle habits from a young age.

Strong Emotional Resilience

Emotional intelligence is nurtured, allowing children to navigate life's emotional challenges with greater resilience and understanding.

Mindful Decision-Making

Holistic parenting promotes mindfulness in daily choices, from food selection to parenting techniques, leading to informed and conscious decision-making.

Family Bond

By emphasizing open communication, understanding, and shared values, holistic parenting fosters a strong family bond that supports a child's growth and development.

Holistic Parenting Resources

Books and Literature

Numerous books, such as "The Holistic Pediatrician" by Kathi Kemper and "Simplicity Parenting" by Kim John Payne, provide guidance on holistic parenting approaches.

Online Communities

Online forums, blogs, and social media groups dedicated to holistic parenting are valuable resources for parents looking to connect, share experiences, and access a wide range of information.

Holistic Parenting Workshops

Holistic parenting workshops, both online and in-person, offer parents the opportunity to learn directly from experts in the field and interact with like-minded individuals.

Pediatric Holistic Health Services

Some healthcare providers and pediatricians specialize in holistic medicine and child wellness. They can offer guidance on a variety of topics, from nutrition to holistic treatments for common childhood ailments.

Holistic Parenting Coaches

Holistic parenting coaches provide personalized guidance and support for parents seeking to implement a holistic parenting approach in their families.

Holistic parenting offers a comprehensive and interconnected approach to raising children that focuses on their physical, emotional, mental, and spiritual well-being.

A variety of resources, from books and online communities to workshops and coaching services, are available to support parents on their holistic parenting journey.

By nurturing well-rounded children who are emotionally resilient, mentally curious, and spiritually aware, holistic parenting contributes to the creation of a future generation that is not only physically healthy but also balanced in all aspects of life.

Holistic Sexuality Workshops: Embracing Intimacy, Mind, and Body

Holistic sexuality workshops represent a unique and increasingly popular approach to sexual education and self-discovery. These workshops go beyond the physical aspects of sexuality and delve into the emotional, mental, and spiritual dimensions of human intimacy. In this book, we will explore the world of holistic sexuality workshops, their fundamental principles, the benefits they offer, and the significance of embracing sexuality from a holistic perspective.

Understanding Holistic Sexuality

Holistic Approach

Holistic sexuality acknowledges that human sexuality encompasses more than just physical acts. It encompasses the interconnectedness of emotions, mental well-being, and spirituality in the realm of intimacy. It views sexual experiences as opportunities for growth, self-discovery, and connection.

Emotional Intelligence

Holistic sexuality encourages individuals to develop emotional intelligence, which enhances their ability to understand, communicate, and connect with their partners on a deeper level. It prioritizes open and honest communication about desires, boundaries, and consent.

Mental and Spiritual Connection

Holistic sexuality explores the mental and spiritual aspects of sexuality. It involves practices like mindfulness, meditation, and self-reflection to enhance self-awareness and to establish a stronger connection with one's partner on all levels.

Benefits of Holistic Sexuality Workshops

Enhanced Intimacy

Holistic sexuality workshops foster a deeper connection between partners. By exploring the emotional and spiritual aspects of sexuality, participants can experience more profound intimacy and emotional bonding.

Improved Communication

Effective communication is essential for a healthy sexual relationship. Holistic sexuality workshops teach participants to express their desires, boundaries, and needs openly, leading to better communication in and out of the bedroom.

Self-Exploration and Self-Acceptance

These workshops encourage individuals to explore their own desires, fantasies, and body in a non-judgmental and accepting environment. This self-exploration can lead to greater self-acceptance and confidence.

Stress Reduction

Mindfulness and relaxation techniques taught in holistic sexuality workshops can reduce stress and anxiety, which often interfere with one's ability to experience pleasure and connection.

Holistic Wellness

Embracing a holistic approach to sexuality can positively impact overall well-being, as it recognizes the interconnectedness of physical, emotional, and mental health with sexual satisfaction.

Key Elements of Holistic Sexuality Workshops

Education

Holistic sexuality workshops provide comprehensive education on anatomy, sexual health, and the emotional and spiritual aspects of sexuality. Participants learn about the body and the mind, as well as communication skills for sexual relationships.

Mindfulness Practices

These workshops often incorporate mindfulness and meditation exercises to help participants become more present and aware during sexual experiences. This can lead to greater sexual satisfaction and emotional connection.

Emotional Intelligence

Emotional intelligence and communication are key components of holistic sexuality workshops. Participants learn how to express their desires, listen to their partners, and establish clear boundaries.

Spiritual Connection

Some workshops explore the spiritual aspects of sexuality, teaching participants to connect with their partners on a deeper level and to understand the role of spirituality in intimacy.

Self-Exploration

Holistic sexuality workshops encourage self-exploration and self-acceptance. Participants are guided to examine their own desires, beliefs, and body image in a supportive and non-judgmental environment.

Holistic Sexuality Workshops in Practice

Finding Workshops

Holistic sexuality workshops are often offered by certified sex therapists, relationship counselors, or holistic wellness professionals. They can be found in wellness centers, online platforms, and retreats.

Group or Individual Sessions

These workshops can be conducted in group settings or as individual sessions, depending on personal preferences and needs.

Inclusivity

Holistic sexuality workshops aim to be inclusive, welcoming participants of all genders, sexual orientations, and relationship dynamics. They respect and celebrate diverse experiences of sexuality.

Holistic sexuality workshops offer a unique opportunity to explore sexuality from a broader perspective, embracing the emotional, mental, and spiritual dimensions of intimacy.

By enhancing emotional intelligence, improving communication, and fostering deeper connections with partners, participants can experience greater intimacy and fulfillment in their sexual relationships.

These workshops are a testament to the evolving field of sexual education, promoting holistic wellness, self-acceptance, and open communication in the realm of human sexuality.

Holistic Skin Care Workshops: Nurturing Skin Naturally

In the pursuit of radiant, healthy skin, a holistic approach has gained increasing popularity. Holistic skin care emphasizes the use of natural and sustainable practices that consider the interconnectedness of the mind, body, and environment. Holistic skin care workshops offer valuable opportunities for individuals to learn about and apply these principles to their skincare routines. This book explores the world of holistic skin care workshops, explaining their core principles, the benefits they offer, and why embracing natural skincare practices is essential for overall well-being.

Holistic Skin Care: An Overview

Holistic Philosophy

Holistic skin care takes a broader perspective on skincare, recognizing that the health and appearance of the skin are influenced by factors like diet, lifestyle, emotions, and the environment. It aims to balance and nourish the skin naturally, addressing the root causes of skin issues, rather than merely treating symptoms.

Natural Ingredients

Holistic skincare emphasizes the use of natural, non-toxic, and sustainable ingredients. It often avoids synthetic chemicals, preservatives, and artificial fragrances that can be harmful to the skin and the environment.

Mind-Body Connection

Holistic skin care recognizes the impact of mental and emotional well-being on the skin. Stress, anxiety, and other emotional factors can affect the skin's health, making stress management an integral part of holistic skincare.

Benefits of Holistic Skin Care Workshops

Healthier Skin

Holistic skin care workshops provide participants with knowledge on natural ingredients and skincare practices that promote healthier, clearer, and more radiant skin.

Nourishment from Within

Holistic skincare encourages a focus on a balanced diet and hydration as essential components of skincare, which contributes to improved skin health from the inside out.

Natural and Non-Toxic Products

Participants learn how to identify and select natural, non-toxic skincare products that are gentle on the skin and environmentally friendly.

Personalized Skincare

Holistic skin care workshops teach participants how to create personalized skincare routines tailored to their unique skin type and concerns.

Emotional Well-Being

Holistic skincare emphasizes emotional well-being and stress reduction, as it acknowledges the impact of stress and emotional factors on the skin's health.

Key Elements of Holistic Skin Care Workshops

Understanding Skin Health

Workshops provide participants with a comprehensive understanding of the skin's structure and function, as well as the common factors that affect its health.

Natural Ingredients

Participants learn about natural ingredients like essential oils, plant extracts, and herbal remedies that can be used to cleanse, moisturize, and protect the skin.

DIY Skincare Recipes

Holistic skin care workshops often include practical demonstrations and hands-on activities to teach participants how to create their own natural skincare products at home, such as cleansers, masks, and serums.

Nutrition and Diet

Participants gain knowledge about the role of nutrition and diet in skincare, understanding how dietary choices can influence skin health and appearance.

Stress Management

Holistic skin care workshops often integrate stress management techniques like mindfulness, meditation, and relaxation exercises to help participants achieve emotional balance, which can benefit their skin.

Holistic Skin Care Workshops in Practice

Finding Workshops

Holistic skin care workshops are offered by skincare professionals, holistic practitioners, wellness centers, and online platforms. Some may be single sessions, while others could span over several weeks or months.

Inclusivity

Holistic skin care workshops are generally inclusive, suitable for individuals with all skin types and concerns. They cater to a diverse range of skin needs and are typically suitable for people of all genders.

Sustainability

Holistic skin care often promotes sustainability and eco-friendliness. Workshops may provide information on choosing eco-conscious skincare products and practices.

Holistic skin care workshops provide a gateway to embracing natural, sustainable, and balanced skincare practices.

By understanding the principles of holistic skin care, including natural ingredients, nutrition, and emotional well-being, participants can achieve healthier, more radiant skin.

These workshops not only promote personal well-being but also contribute to a more environmentally friendly approach to skincare. Embracing holistic skincare practices is an essential step towards achieving the ultimate goal of glowing, healthy skin that reflects overall well-being.

Holistic Space Design: Crafting Energetically Balanced and Harmonious Living Environments

The spaces in which we live, work, and play have a profound impact on our well-being and overall quality of life. Holistic space design is an approach that takes into account not only aesthetics and functionality but also the energetic and psychological aspects of our surroundings. This book explores the world of holistic space design, outlining its core principles, the benefits it offers, and how to create spaces that are harmonious and energetically balanced.

The Essence of Holistic Space Design

Holistic Approach

Holistic space design recognizes the interconnection between the physical, emotional, mental, and spiritual aspects of our lives and living environments. It seeks to create spaces that support and nurture the whole person.

Energy Flow

The concept of energy flow, often referred to as chi or prana, plays a pivotal role in holistic space design. Spaces are arranged to promote the free flow of positive energy and to remove blockages that may impede well-being.

Emotional Impact

Holistic design takes into account the emotional responses that spaces evoke. It aims to create environments that induce positive emotions, reduce stress, and foster a sense of security and contentment.

Benefits of Holistic Space Design

Improved Well-Being

Energetically balanced and harmonious spaces have a positive impact on mental and emotional well-being. They can reduce stress, enhance mood, and promote relaxation.

Enhanced Productivity

Thoughtful space design can boost productivity and creativity by minimizing distractions, creating

134

an organized and inspiring workspace, and promoting focus and concentration.

Better Sleep

Bedroom design that prioritizes relaxation and tranquility can lead to improved sleep quality, which is essential for overall health and vitality.

Stronger Connection with Nature

Holistic design often incorporates elements from the natural world, such as indoor plants, natural light, and sustainable materials, fostering a deeper connection to the environment.

Energy Flow and Balance

Creating energetically balanced spaces can positively affect the physical and emotional health of the inhabitants. Proper energy flow can improve vitality, health, and overall life satisfaction.

Key Elements of Holistic Space Design

Layout and Flow

Holistic space design considers the layout of rooms, ensuring they facilitate the free flow of energy and movement. Furniture placement and room organization are critical components.

Color Psychology

The use of color is a crucial element in holistic design. Different colors can evoke various emotions, and choosing the right colors for a space is essential for creating the desired ambiance.

Sustainable and Natural Materials

The use of eco-friendly and natural materials like wood, stone, and organic fabrics is a hallmark of holistic design, contributing to a healthier and more sustainable environment.

Balance and Harmony

Holistic space design incorporates principles of balance and harmony in its aesthetic choices. These principles apply to everything from furniture arrangement to decorative elements.

Mindfulness and Clutter Reduction

The reduction of clutter and the incorporation of mindfulness practices contribute to the creation of serene and balanced spaces. Clutter-free environments allow the energy to flow freely.

Holistic Space Design in Practice

Finding Design Professionals

Holistic interior designers and Feng Shui consultants are professionals who specialize in holistic space design. Seek their expertise to help you create energetically balanced spaces.

DIY Holistic Design

You can also implement holistic design principles on your own. Start by decluttering, choosing natural and sustainable materials, and creating balanced layouts.

Mindful Practices

Incorporating mindfulness practices like meditation and grounding exercises in your daily life can enhance your connection with your living space and increase its positive impact on your well-being.

Personalization

Holistic design is highly personalized. Consider your unique needs, preferences, and the specific energy of your space when making design choices.

Holistic space design is a holistic and comprehensive approach to creating living environments that are not only visually pleasing but also energetically balanced and harmonious.

By integrating the principles of energy flow, emotional impact, and mindfulness, these spaces promote well-being, reduce stress, and enhance productivity.

Whether you enlist the help of professionals or undertake the process yourself, embracing holistic space design can lead to living environments that nourish the mind, body, and soul, fostering overall well-being and contentment.

Holistic Veterinary Care: Nurturing Animal Wellness from a Wholesome Perspective

The world of veterinary medicine has evolved beyond conventional treatments and is embracing a more holistic approach to animal health and well-being. Holistic veterinary care extends beyond traditional medical practices to consider the physical, emotional, and mental aspects of an animal's health. In this book, we will explore the world of holistic veterinary care, outlining its fundamental principles, the benefits it offers, and the significance of applying holistic principles to ensure the health and well-being of animals.

The Essence of Holistic Veterinary Care

Holistic Approach

Holistic veterinary care is rooted in the philosophy that animals, like humans, are complex beings whose health is influenced by interconnected factors, including physical, emotional, and mental well-being. Holistic veterinarians aim to treat the whole animal, rather than just the symptoms of a disease or ailment.

Integrative Techniques

Holistic veterinary care combines various techniques and therapies, including traditional Western medicine, acupuncture, chiropractic care, herbal remedies, nutrition, and complementary therapies like massage and energy healing.

Benefits of Holistic Veterinary Care

Comprehensive Wellness

Holistic veterinary care promotes the overall well-being of animals. By considering physical, emotional, and mental health, it provides a more complete approach to animal health.

Personalized Treatment

Holistic veterinarians develop customized treatment plans tailored to each animal's unique needs, taking into account their medical history, lifestyle, and emotional state.

Minimized Side Effects

Holistic therapies often use natural and gentle treatments, minimizing the risk of adverse side effects or harm to the animal's body.

Emotional Support

Holistic veterinarians recognize the emotional well-being of animals and work to reduce stress and anxiety, which can positively impact an animal's physical health.

Prevention and Wellness

Holistic veterinary care also focuses on preventive measures and wellness programs, helping animals maintain good health and prevent diseases.

Key Elements of Holistic Veterinary Care

Comprehensive Evaluation

Holistic veterinarians conduct in-depth assessments of the animal's physical, emotional, and mental well-being. They take into account the animal's history, behaviors, and lifestyle.

Natural and Alternative Therapies

Holistic veterinary care includes a wide range of natural and alternative therapies, such as acupuncture, chiropractic care, herbal medicine, homeopathy, and energy healing.

Nutrition

Nutrition plays a crucial role in holistic veterinary care. Holistic veterinarians often prescribe individualized diets that support the animal's specific health needs.

Emotional Health

Holistic veterinarians are attuned to the emotional health of animals and work to alleviate stress and anxiety through gentle, non-invasive therapies.

Preventive Medicine

Holistic veterinary care encourages preventive measures, including vaccinations, parasite control, and lifestyle adjustments, to maintain the animal's health and well-being.

Holistic Veterinary Care in Practice

Finding Holistic Veterinarians

To access holistic veterinary care, look for holistic veterinarians in your area. These professionals are typically certified in holistic and integrative medicine, and you can find them through online directories and word-of-mouth recommendations.

Integrating Holistic Principles at Home

You can also apply holistic principles to your pet's life by considering their emotional needs, providing a balanced diet, and creating a low-stress environment.

Communication with Your Veterinarian

If you choose to integrate holistic practices with conventional veterinary care, ensure open communication with your veterinarian. Discuss your pet's specific needs and collaborate to create the most suitable treatment plan.

Holistic veterinary care is a multifaceted approach that considers the overall well-being of animals. By embracing the principles of holistic care, we can promote not only the physical health but also the emotional and mental well-being of our beloved pets.

Whether you choose to consult a holistic veterinarian or integrate holistic principles into your pet's life at home, the goal remains the same: to ensure that our animal companions lead happy, healthy, and well-rounded lives.

Holistic Weight Management: Nurturing Wellness, Mind, and Body

In an era where the quest for healthy weight and wellness is more prevalent than ever, holistic weight management emerges as a comprehensive approach that goes beyond simply shedding pounds. Holistic weight management focuses on nurturing overall well-being by considering not only the physical aspect of weight but also the emotional, mental, and spiritual dimensions of health. In this book, we will explore the world of holistic weight management, its core principles, the benefits it offers, and how to approach weight management with a holistic perspective.

The Essence of Holistic Weight Management

Holistic Approach

Holistic weight management recognizes that an individual's overall health and well-being are intertwined with their body weight. It considers the interconnectedness of physical, emotional, mental, and spiritual aspects of life.

Mind-Body-Soul Connection

Holistic weight management addresses not only physical health but also the emotional and mental states of individuals. It acknowledges the role of emotional well-being, self-acceptance, and personal growth in the weight management journey.

Long-Term Wellness

Holistic weight management aims for lasting and sustainable results, shifting the focus from quick fixes to developing healthy habits that promote overall well-being.

Benefits of Holistic Weight Management

Sustainable Weight Loss

By addressing emotional and mental aspects of weight management, holistic approaches help individuals achieve and maintain their weight goals more sustainably.

Improved Emotional Health

Holistic weight management nurtures emotional well-being and self-acceptance, reducing the risk of disordered eating and improving the relationship individuals have with their bodies.

Enhanced Mental Resilience

Holistic approaches teach stress management techniques, mindfulness, and coping strategies that can improve mental resilience and reduce emotional eating.

Holistic Wellness

Holistic weight management contributes to holistic wellness, considering the interconnectedness of physical, emotional, mental, and spiritual health.

Empowerment

Holistic weight management empowers individuals to take charge of their health and develop a deeper understanding of themselves and their bodies.

147

Key Elements of Holistic Weight Management

Mindful Eating

Holistic weight management emphasizes mindful eating, which involves paying attention to the taste, texture, and sensations of food. This practice encourages individuals to listen to their body's hunger and fullness cues.

Emotional Well-Being

Addressing emotional well-being is a crucial component of holistic weight management. Strategies for stress management, emotional self-care, and improved body image are integrated into the approach.

Balanced Nutrition

Holistic weight management promotes balanced and sustainable nutrition. It discourages extreme diets and instead focuses on whole, nutrient-dense foods and portion control.

Physical Activity

Exercise is a key element, but the approach is more holistic, encompassing not just the physical benefits of activity but also the emotional and mental rewards.

Lifestyle and Behavior Change

Holistic weight management emphasizes developing sustainable lifestyle habits and behaviors. It focuses on setting realistic goals, tracking progress, and adjusting strategies when necessary.

Holistic Weight Management in Practice

Professional Guidance

To benefit from holistic weight management, consider consulting with professionals such as holistic nutritionists, wellness coaches, therapists, or registered dietitians who are trained in holistic approaches.

Self-Care and Mindfulness

Incorporating self-care practices, mindfulness, and stress management techniques into daily life can help individuals embrace a more holistic approach to weight management.

Support and Community

Joining a supportive community or finding an accountability partner can be instrumental in achieving holistic weight management goals. Connecting with like-minded individuals can provide motivation and a sense of belonging.

Education and Self-Reflection

Continue to educate yourself about holistic weight management and engage in self-reflection to understand your emotional and mental relationship with food, exercise, and overall well-being.

Holistic weight management is a comprehensive approach to achieving and maintaining a healthy weight. It emphasizes the interconnectedness of physical, emotional, mental, and spiritual aspects of health, aiming to promote overall well-being and lasting results. Whether you consult with professionals, integrate holistic practices into your daily life, or seek support from a community, embracing a holistic perspective on weight management is a vital step toward achieving a balanced and fulfilling life.

Holistic Writing Classes: Unleashing Creativity and Spirituality in Writing

Writing is not just an act of putting words on paper; it is a journey of self-discovery, creativity, and expression. Holistic writing classes offer a unique perspective that extends beyond the technicalities of writing to explore deeper themes of spirituality, mindfulness, and interconnectedness. In this book, we will delve into the world of holistic writing classes, exploring their core principles, the benefits they offer, and how they empower writers to infuse their work with holistic and spiritual themes.

The Essence of Holistic Writing

Holistic Approach

Holistic writing embraces the idea that writing is not isolated from the writer's inner world. It acknowledges the interplay between the writer's thoughts, emotions, and spirit and their creative expression.

Mind-Body-Soul Connection

Holistic writing delves into the mind-body-soul connection. It encourages writers to explore their inner landscapes, emotions, and spiritual beliefs to create more authentic and meaningful works.

Self-Discovery and Personal Growth

Holistic writing classes offer a platform for self-discovery, personal growth, and self-expression. Writers explore their own beliefs, experiences, and worldviews, allowing for greater depth and authenticity in their writing.

Benefits of Holistic Writing Classes

Enhanced Creativity

Holistic writing classes inspire creativity by guiding writers to tap into their innermost thoughts, feelings, and beliefs, unleashing new depths of imagination and storytelling.

Personal Empowerment

Exploring one's spiritual and holistic beliefs can empower writers to find their unique voice and express their authentic selves.

Emotional Well-Being

Holistic writing classes provide a space for emotional expression, self-reflection, and catharsis, supporting emotional well-being and self-awareness.

Deeper Connection

Writers who delve into spiritual and holistic themes in their work can create a stronger connection with readers who share similar beliefs and experiences.

Personal Growth

Holistic writing encourages personal growth by guiding writers to explore and understand their own spirituality, beliefs, and values, which can have a profound impact on their lives.

Key Elements of Holistic Writing Classes

Self-Exploration

Holistic writing classes emphasize self-exploration and introspection. Writers are encouraged to delve into their own beliefs, experiences, and inner worlds.

Mindfulness and Presence

Mindfulness practices are often integrated into these classes, helping writers become more present and focused in their writing, leading to richer and more meaningful content.

Spiritual Themes

Holistic writing classes explore a wide range of spiritual themes, including mindfulness, meditation, personal growth, self-discovery, and interconnectedness.

Authenticity

Holistic writing encourages authenticity by guiding writers to draw on their personal experiences and beliefs to create more relatable and impactful stories.

Creative Exercises

These classes often include creative exercises and prompts that help writers access their inner creativity and explore spiritual and holistic themes in their work.

Holistic Writing Classes in Practice

Finding Classes

Holistic writing classes are offered in various formats, including in-person workshops, online courses, and self-study programs. Consider your learning preferences and availability when seeking classes.

Writing Communities

Joining writing communities and groups that focus on holistic and spiritual themes can be a great way to connect with like-minded writers, share experiences, and find support and inspiration.

Personal Journaling

Engaging in personal journaling with a holistic and spiritual perspective can be an informal way to explore your own beliefs and experiences, which can then be incorporated into your writing.

Reflect and Share

After taking holistic writing classes, take time to reflect on your experiences and personal growth. Share your work with others to inspire and connect with fellow writers who resonate with your spiritual themes.

Holistic writing classes offer a unique and enriching approach to writing that explores spirituality, mindfulness, and interconnectedness.

By guiding writers to delve into their inner worlds, beliefs, and experiences, these classes empower writers to create more authentic and meaningful works.

Whether you choose to participate in formal classes, join writing communities, or engage in personal journaling, embracing a holistic perspective in your writing can lead to personal growth, self-discovery, and a deeper connection with your readers.

Holistic Writing Retreats: Nurturing Creative and Spiritual Expression

The art of writing transcends the mere arrangement of words on a page; it is a deeply personal and spiritual journey that allows writers to express their innermost thoughts and emotions. Holistic writing retreats offer writers a unique and transformative experience, blending creative expression with spiritual exploration. In this book, we will explore the world of holistic writing retreats, uncovering their principles, the benefits they offer, and how they empower writers to nurture their creative and spiritual selves.

The Essence of Holistic Writing Retreats

Holistic Approach

Holistic writing retreats adopt a perspective that goes beyond the mechanics of writing. They emphasize the interconnectedness of the physical, emotional, mental, and spiritual aspects of the writing process.

Mind-Body-Spirit Connection

Holistic writing encourages writers to explore the mind-body-spirit connection in their work. This approach recognizes that writing is a deeply personal and spiritual journey, offering a way to express one's beliefs, emotions, and soul.

Self-Discovery and Growth

Holistic writing retreats are designed to foster self-discovery and personal growth. They invite writers to delve into their own beliefs, experiences, and inner landscapes, which can lead to a richer, more authentic writing style.

Benefits of Holistic Writing Retreats

Enhanced Creativity

Holistic writing retreats inspire creativity by guiding writers to explore their innermost thoughts, feelings, and spiritual beliefs. This process unleashes a wellspring of imagination and storytelling.

Personal Empowerment

Writers attending holistic retreats often emerge with a deep sense of empowerment. By exploring their spiritual and holistic beliefs, they can discover their unique voices and express their authentic selves.

Emotional Well-Being

These retreats provide a space for emotional expression, self-reflection, and catharsis. Writers can find emotional healing, increased self-awareness, and improved well-being through their writing.

Deeper Connection

Writers who delve into spiritual and holistic themes in their work can establish a stronger connection with readers who share similar beliefs and experiences.

Personal Growth

Holistic writing retreats encourage personal growth by guiding writers to explore and understand their own spirituality, beliefs, and values, which can have a profound impact on their lives.

Key Elements of Holistic Writing Retreats

Self-Exploration

Holistic writing retreats emphasize self-exploration and introspection. Writers are encouraged to delve into their own beliefs, experiences, and inner worlds.

Mindfulness and Presence

Mindfulness practices are often an integral part of these retreats, helping writers become more present and focused in their writing. This enhances the depth and authenticity of their work.

Spiritual Themes

Holistic writing retreats explore a wide range of spiritual themes, including mindfulness, meditation, personal growth, self-discovery, and interconnectedness.

Authenticity

Holistic writing emphasizes authenticity by guiding writers to draw on their personal experiences and beliefs to create relatable and impactful stories.

Creative Exercises

These retreats often include creative exercises and prompts that help writers access their inner creativity and explore spiritual and holistic themes in their work.

Holistic Writing Retreats in Practice

Finding Retreats

Holistic writing retreats are offered in various formats, including in-person events, online programs, and self-directed retreats. Consider your learning preferences, availability, and goals when seeking retreats.

Retreat Centers and Communities

Retreat centers and writing communities that focus on holistic and spiritual themes can be excellent resources for finding holistic writing retreats. They can connect you with like-minded individuals and provide guidance in your journey.

Personal Retreats

If attending a formal retreat is not possible, consider creating your own personal writing retreat at home or in a location that inspires you. Implement mindfulness practices, explore spiritual themes, and engage in self-exploration as part of your retreat.

Reflect and Share

After participating in holistic writing retreats, take time to reflect on your experiences and personal growth. Share your work with others to inspire and connect with fellow writers who resonate with your spiritual themes.

Holistic writing retreats offer a unique and transformative experience for writers seeking to nurture their creative and spiritual selves. By blending creative expression with spiritual exploration, these retreats empower writers to embark on a journey of self-discovery, self-expression, and personal growth. Whether you choose to attend formal retreats, create personal writing retreats, or engage in self-guided practices, embracing a holistic perspective in your writing can lead to personal fulfillment and a deeper connection with your readers.

Conclusion

As we draw the curtains on our exploration within "Holistic Wellness: Whole Wellness & Wonderful Well-being," it's essential to recognize that the holistic journey is as diverse and unique as each individual. The glimpses provided in this book serve as starting points, beckoning you to delve deeper, ask questions, and find the holistic practices that resonate most with your personal journey.

The world of holistic living is vast and ever-evolving. While this book offers a curated introduction, the true essence of holistic well-being lies in continuous learning, exploration, and self-reflection. It's about listening intently to your body, honoring your emotions, nurturing your mind, and seeking spiritual alignment while understanding that perfection is not the goal—balance is.

Remember, holistic living is not a destination but a journey. It's a path that encourages mindfulness, compassion, and a deeper connection to the world around us.

As you move forward, let the insights from "Whole Wellness & Wonderful Well-being" serve as gentle reminders and guiding lights. Seek out further knowledge, engage with communities that share your interests, and always trust your intuition as you navigate the diverse landscape of holistic well-being.

In closing, may your holistic journey be filled with discovery, growth, and a more profound sense of harmony. Let the principles and practices you've explored within this book inspire and guide you as you embark on this enriching path toward complete well-being. Here's to a life lived holistically, with awareness, intention, and joy.

About the Author

Sydney Brown has spent over thirty-five years in the business world and later in the corporate world. She has learned what works and what doesn't when the goal is to get out of the stale, vanilla world of the generations before us.

She believes that each person has at least one successful business, one book, and one grand adventure in them, but most people don't know how to figure out their best fit, so they stay where they are.

She is a best-selling author, speaker, and coach, helping people reach out of their current situation and reinvent themselves so they can do more than exist and survive while in this great space.

Personally, she's a mom of two adulting children and proudly owns the title of "Crazy Cat Lady" among her friends. After too many years of avoiding living life, she is on a mission to help others identify and begin their own "Great Ascension."

Let's Connect

If you've enjoyed this book, you'll love what else is ahead!

Start out at https://beyourownsolution.com/ and see what you can look forward to.

We have courses, certifications, and life and business focused free groups!

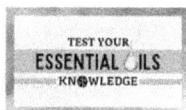

Free Essential Oil Quiz
Click to Sign Up

Aromatherapy Alchemy: Gateway to Wellness
Click to Sign Up

Project Flow Mastery: Universal Laws at Work
Click to Sign Up

Life in Flow: Path Toward Personal Wellness

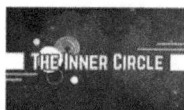

The Inner Circle

Free Groups:

https://www.facebook.com/groups/fundsfriends futures

https://www.facebook.com/groups/shifttimes

Also From TLM Publishing House

FICTION –

Sydney Brown Presents Series

https://www.amazon.com/dp/B0BSBT36HN

The Mall Cadet Series

https://www.amazon.com/gp/product/B0B66M DK3T

All In or Nothing Series

https://www.amazon.com/dp/B0B7FW9W8M

The 7 Wishes Series

https://www.amazon.com/dp/B0B62XJY59

The Deception Series

https://www.amazon.com/dp/B0B5RNQMF1

The Forbidden Love Series (18+)

https://www.amazon.com/dp/B0B5SX24SX

NONFICTION –

How to Start It Series

https://www.amazon.com/dp/B09Y2QHDPM

Aromatherapy Alchemy

https://www.amazon.com/dp/B0CJ5DD5C1

www.ingramcontent.com/pod-product-compliance
Lightning Source LLC
Chambersburg PA
CBHW061144040426
42445CB00013B/1542